To all mothers:

Those queens of our hearts

whose simple and generous

cooking inspires and

sustains us.

Georges Blanc

Simple French Cooking
Recipes from our mothers' kitchens

Georges Blanc
Coco Jobard

Photography by
Jean-François Rivière

Styling by
Marie-France Michalon

Foreword

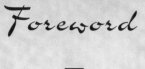

When Georges Blanc asked me collaborate with him on a book dedicated to his grandmother Elisa, known as Mère Blanc, and to several other mothers, I agreed immediately. I have always felt an affinity with that generation of women cooks—probably the last—who enjoyed spending hours, perhaps whole days at the stove. I inherited this passion from my own mother, Madeleine Jobard and from my grandmother, Marie Vieille-Girardet. These women taught me the special cooking techniques and the methods of preparation that distinguish the cuisine of my part of France, the Franche-Comté: Skimming the scum from a pan of simmering wild blackberry jelly; cleaning black trumpet, blue foot, and *gris-de-sapin* mushrooms picked from the meadows; skinning frogs fished from my grandmother Marie's lake in Hyan's Dell; carefully collecting the golden cream off the top of the still-warm milk; kneading brioche dough for hours on Sundays. In turn, I have tried to pass this wealth of knowledge onto those around me.

Elisa Blanc, Eugénie Brazier, Gisèle Crouzier, Catarina-Elena Barale, Annette Poulard, and countless other mothers are all a part of this tradition. They understand the intuitive and organic nature of cooking. A talent for and understanding of food has been passed onto

Madeleine Jobard in 1932.

them from their mothers, who had learned from their grandmothers, who in turn learned from watching their own mothers... These mothers have inspired and paved the way for the great chefs of today.

Their influence lives on, as it is the real basis of French cuisine. Hélène Chazal, Véronique Dauphin, Lulu, Marie-Claude Gracia, Jocelyne Lotz-Choquart, Reine Sammut, and countless others who work their magic in the kitchen continue this tradition of quietly producing fabulous food using the best local produce. They treat their ingredients with respect and possess a fundamental understanding of how to harmonize flavors. Danièle Mazet-Delpeuch, the first and only female cook at the Élysée Palace, the home of France's president, declared that "the term *mère* may no longer be used, but it continues to embody a very specific idea." Fresh ingredients, careful blending of flavors, simple methods of preparation, and slow cooking over properly controlled heat are all patiently combined through a love of food. After all, cooking is about charm, seduction, sharing, and, above all, loving those for whom you prepare the food. What better gift is there than to prepare and share a meal?

Colette Jobard a.k.a. Coco Jobard

Contents

La Mère Adrienne

Les Mères Allard

La Mère Barale

La Mère Blanc

La Mère Brazier

Once upon a time there were the mothers

La Mère Bourgeois

La Mère Castaing

La Mère Crouzier

La Mère Léa

La Mère Poulard

The Mères of Lyons

The talented women chefs who were practicing in Lyons at the end of the nineteenth century were affectionately nicknamed *mères*, mothers. Their reputations rested on their mastery of *cuisine bourgeoise*, home cooking raised to a higher level by the application of passion and perfectionism. Curnonsky, "prince of the gourmets," declared that, "without resorting to artifice, this cuisine attains that peak of artistry: simplicity." An avid proponent of female chefs, he had always been a devotee of the women whom he called the "priestesses of the table." The cooking of the *mères* came from their own hearts and made their customers' hearts leap for joy. Certainly, they did not cook to impress. Their generally dour demeanor did not allow for frills. The joy that they lavished on their food, the comforting, motherly warmth of their simple and honest cuisine made them queens—queens of hearts.

Lyons' fortunate geographical location was probably the reason it became the "cradle" of the *mères*. Bridging northern and southern France, Lyons is surrounded by regions famous for their gourmet heritage: Bresse, Dombes, Franche-Comté, Burgundy, Bugey, Dauphiné, Velay, Bourbon, and Forez. This has made sure that cooks in Lyons have always had access to a wide variety of high-quality, fresh ingredients.

The first reference to a *mère* of Lyons dates from 1759. A sign for an inn by the Rhône river refers to "La Mère Guy" whose specialty was an exquisite eel stew. A century later, La Génie, her granddaughter, was being called "Mère Guy." A rosy-faced woman with her hair in ringlets and a sharp turn of phrase, she oversaw the cooking range alongside her sister. Her menu listed a number of regional specialties, including her grandmother's renowned eel stew. At about the same time, "Mère Brigousse" was enjoying popularity in the Charpenes quarter of the city with a dish called Venus's breasts. These enormous dumplings were favorites with bachelors celebrating a stag night.

La Mère Filloux

Françoise Fayolle, better known as Mère Filloux, was the first of the famous *mères* whose recipes continue to be used today and whose style influenced the most prestigious chefs of the region.

One of the 500,000 chickens which Mère Filloux carved at the restaurant tables. Each table was allocated a whole chicken, even if it was occupied by only a single diner.

"Learning how to make a perfect dish requires years of experience," claimed Mère Filloux. "I have never made more than about four or five dishes throughout my life. I know how to cook them, and I will never make any others." But what dishes! Creamy soup with truffles, poached chicken, also flavored with truffles (the specialty of the house), artichoke hearts stuffed with *foie gras*, quenelles baked in crayfish butter, and spiny lobster *à l'américaine* (with shallots, tomatoes, wine, and brandy).

In 1890, the young Françoise Fayolle moved to Lyons from Cunlhat, in the Puy-de-Dôme region. Gaston Eymard, the director of the La France insurance company, and one of the city's foremost gourmets, hired her as his cook. There she learned excellent homestyle cooking. She developed a repertoire of dishes, which she would be able to use when, after marrying Louis Filloux, she bought a modest restaurant at 73 Rue Duquesne. Her fame spread as much for her performance at the table as for her food: "Mère Filloux was a short, compact woman in a starched enveloping apron with a short, narrow but formidable knife which she brandished as she moved from table to table carving each chicken. That was her pleasure and her privilege which she never relinquished to another. She was an expert carver. She placed a fork in the chicken once and for all. Neither she nor the plate moved, the legs and the wings fell, the two breasts in less than a matter of minutes, and then she was gone. A whole chicken was always dedicated to each table, even if there was only one person at it. Not to have any small economies gave style to the restaurant. She was an artist," wrote Alice B. Toklas, who, with her friend and companion Gertrude Stein, was a frequent visitor to Mère Filloux's restaurant.

Mère Filloux had carved half a million chickens by 1925, the year that she retired, and she had only ever owned two knives.

A stack of charlotte molds waits patiently to be slipped into the oven.

The restaurant, taken over by her son-in-law Désiré Fréchin, was destroyed after World War II. However, Mère Filloux, who tantalized the palates of gourmets with her inimitable fine lunches and dinners for 3.50 French francs, is still remembered as a part of the history of great French cuisine.

La Mère Brazier

Eugènie Brazier started working for Mère Filloux in order to supplement her family income and raise her son Gaston. Born in 1895 in a small village near Bourg-en-Bresse, she spent the first years of her life on her parents' farm. After her mother's death, she worked on the farm. An unmarried mother at 21, she left for Lyons, where she worked as a maid for the Milliats, a family who manufactured pasta. It was at their rented summer villa in Cannes that Eugènie's talent for cooking first became apparent. "I learned how to cook by doing everything very simply," she explained. By the age of five, she had already mastered the two recipes for pies that her mother regularly prepared—one was a type of cream dessert, *béchamel* sauce poured onto a pie dough base; the other was a pie shell filled with cream and onions softened in a little butter. She also made bread and milk soup: "Such a simple dish. Take a broth of leeks and other vegetables simmered in milk and water. Vigorously whisk several egg whites into the broth, then pour a little of the liquid onto the yolks. Mix well, then pour the soup over pieces of bread arranged in a tureen. Let rest for a while, then enjoy."

When Mère Filloux became too old to supervise her kitchen—but not too old to stop the ceremonial carving at the tables—she passed the responsibility onto Eugènie. It was not a painless transition. Mère Filloux found it hard to accept Eugènie's gifts as a cook, and endlessly criticized and nagged her. Eugènie tolerated this treatment; she could not afford to lose her job.

Mère Filloux's restaurant closed for a month in August each year and Eugènie used this opportunity to take up additional employment at the *Brasserie du Dragon*. This caused some confusion for the patrons. They assumed that the *Brasserie du Dragon* must be Mère Filloux's new restaurant if Eugènie Brazier was tending the ovens there. One day, attempting to compliment her, one of Mère Filloux's regulars reported that he "ate a marvelous roast chicken and delicious green beans [at the Brasserie]." An angry

Eugènie Brazier glows with the pure pleasure of spending her days actively involved in her passion—cooking.

Mère Filloux retorted, "But she is only a pot scrubber." "Then it is an even greater credit to her," replied the bemused customer.

In 1921, Eugènie was able to buy 12 Rue Royale, an old grocery which had once been a *porte-pot* (literally "carry-pitcher"), the Lyons term for a bistro, so called because business in that city was always conducted around a 2-cup pitcher of Brouilly, Fleurie, Morgon, or Juliènas wine. Eugènie was able to set up her restaurant for 12,000 French francs, a relatively small sum of money at the time. Her former employer at the *Brasserie du Dragon* helped her with the purchase of wine and supplies. The restaurant was tiny, only 15 covers, and primarily patronized by doctors and a few pensioners.

Eugènie was asked to provide a cold buffet for everyone taking part in the Spido, an annual horse race sponsored by Spidoléine, a brand of cooking oil. Astonished and delighted by her food, the race's director asked her to travel to Paris and cook the racing banquet every year.

Her reputation was established. Édouard Herriot, the mayor of Lyons and president of the city council, ate at her restaurant increasingly often. The news spread rapidly by word of mouth and her clientele increased. She opened a second dining room and, later, a private salon and two little rooms upstairs.

A victim of her own success, Eugènie was forced to work harder and harder until she became completely exhausted. Mère Brazier was happy to stop and let her son, Gaston, take over the restaurant. She moved to Luère, a village 2,600 feet up in the hills about 12 miles from Lyons. She had purchased, for next to nothing, some land and a decrepit wooden cottage with no gas, water, or electricity. In 1932, after a great deal of work, she opened her second restaurant there. The Michelin judges

A small soup bowl with lion's head handles holds Mère Brazier's tasty *Gratinée Lyonnaise* (onion soup gratinée).

immediately awarded her two stars. The following year, the guide awarded three stars for the restaurant in Luère and another three for the original restaurant in the Rue Royale. Mère Brazier thus became the first woman chef to have been awarded "six stars" at once by Michelin.

The chalet-restaurant in Luère no longer exists. The restaurant at 12 Rue Royale continues to operate under its original red and white "Mère Brazier" sign. It is expertly run by Jacotte, Eugènie's granddaughter and the daughter of Carmen and Gaston Brazier. She is addressed as *Mademoiselle*. "It runs in the family. Like my grandmother, I have never married," she explains. She faithfully continues her grandmother's tradition.

La Mère Bourgeois

A contemporary of Mère Brazier, Marie Bourgeois, born Humbert in 1870, served excellent food at reasonable prices. In October 1922, she received the first ever diploma granted by the exclusive and secretive *Club des Cents*. This club had been formed ten years earlier by three passionate gourmets who wanted to battle against declining standards in French cuisine. Curnonsky described the club as "half sporting and half gastronomic. To join, one must be willing to travel huge distances and have a proven love of the good life." On September 1, 1924,

Mère Bourgeios became the first woman to receive the highest culinary prize in France. It was awarded in Paris on Bresse Day during the fall exhibition at the Grand Palais. Her achievements culminated with the three Michelin stars that she held from 1933 until her death in 1937. A towering figure in French gastronomy, Mère Bourgeois acquired a worldwide reputation without ever leaving the confines of her kitchen.

Marie was one of eight children. As was the custom of the time, at 16 she left the village where she was born to go into service with an affluent

Marie Bourgeois stands in front of her coal-fired range from which emerged such delicacies as her warm pâté of foie gras and truffles.

14

family. She cooked for the family and traveled with them as they moved from Lyons to Paris, from spa towns to fashionable resorts. At some point during her travels, she met her future husband, André Bourgeois.

In 1908, the young couple bought an old coaching inn in Priay, a large village 30 miles from Lyons, not far off the main route from Lyons to Geneva. The nearby River Ain yielded beautiful fresh fish and the area was full of game, such as pheasant, partridge, and grouse, which Marie cooked with flair. Her sumptuous lark pâté soon drew the attention of the local hunters. The reputation of Mère Bourgeois' inn began to grow.

Édouard Herriot, a keen angler, visited the inn at Priay and recommended it to his numerous friends and family. Princes, kings, and grandees all made the pilgrimage to savor the incomparable first-class cuisine. On September 28, 1934, eleven days before he was assassinated alongside King Alexander of Yugoslavia in Marcella, Louis Barthou, the French Minister of Foreign Affairs, wrote: "If the League of Nations were to meet around Mère Bourgeois' tables, it would be the happiest and most unified of Leagues. Perhaps the 'bourgeois' style is not to everyone's taste. Too bad for them. I have just eaten a lunch that can be summed up in one word—marvelous."

Warm pâté with foie gras and truffles, chicken with tarragon, chicken poached with morels, poultry terrine with pistachios and aged Armagnac brandy, roast farmed pigeons and guinea fowls competed with salmon trout or char served simply with a foaming butter sauce. Mère Bourgeois' style of cooking complemented the superb quality of

the ingredients available in Bugey. According to Curnonsky, Bugey "is the birthplace of the fine food and great traditions of French cuisine…," and the simplest dishes deserved as much notice as the most ambitious and elaborate ones.

Marie Bourgeois died at her range on August 2, 1937. Her husband André and her only child, Thérèse Rollin, continued to run the inn successfully for several years, cooking Marie's recipes. In 1951, Georges Berger took over the business. He has maintained Mère Bourgeois' tradition. Today, a chef from Dijon, Hervé Rodriguez, oversees the kitchen and he continues to make stylish versions of Marie's warm pâté of foie gras and truffles.

The indispensable and robust enameled cast-iron dishes that were used to cook fish *meunière*, frog legs in frothy herb butter, and the famous quenelles that were caramelized with a salamander. Mère Blanc called these the hardworking dishes.

La Mère Léa

Léa is the last of the Lyons *mères*, as such. Phillipe Rabatel, her successor and the owner of the restaurant since 1980, remembers her as "an original, slightly crazy and authoritarian, but her cooking was so marvelous that [her behavior] did not matter."

Born in Creusot in 1908, Léa, like most of the *mères*, spent her adolescence working in grand houses. Later, she cooked at a restaurant on Rue Tupin for four years. Then, in 1943, she opened *La Voûte* at a site along the Rhône that was shaded by mulberry trees. At that time, her specialty was a delicious and lavish sauerkraut. When other brasseries in Lyons put the dish on their menus, she stopped serving it and perfected regional specialties, such as *tablier de sapeur* (marinated, crumbed tripe which is fried and served with a chervil sauce), pike quenelles, Lyons salad (a cold plate of cervelat, cold cooked sausage, slices of bacon, and calf's foot), tripe with onions, chicken

Léa in her cook's uniform. A woman to her fingertips, Léa "would paint her nails bright red," reported Jacotte Brazier, who was fascinated by the coquetry of this *mère*.

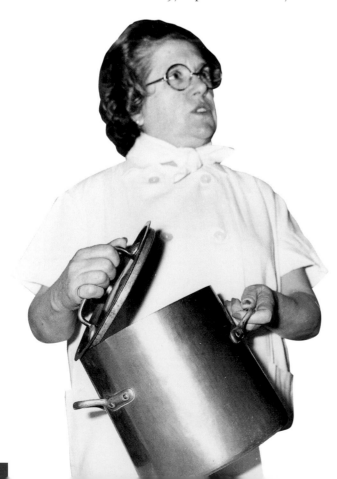

with a vinegar sauce, *cervelle de canuts*—literally Lyonnais silk weavers' brains, but actually fresh herbed cheese—and baked cardoon with bone marrow (in winter). Her famous *bugnes*, crisp, fluffy fritters, were served as a fitting conclusion to the meals.

As she bought ingredients at the Quai Saint-Antoine market every morning, the stall-holders would shout, "Watch out! Here comes Mère Léa." She had a reputation for demanding the highest quality fresh produce. Her hampers full of freshly picked salads, extra thick crème fraîche, milk and freshly churned butter, farmhouse cow's milk and goat cheeses from Dombes and the hills around Lyons, and wild mushrooms, Léa would reply, as she pulled her old hand cart, by indicating a hand-written sign proclaiming,

16

"weak woman but powerful mouth." She was maliciously keen to point out that "mouth" referred to her hard-to-please palate.

La Voûte had neither a printed menu nor set meals. Léa, in her apron, sporting a dishtowel in one hand and a fork in the other, told diners the specialties of the day. The atmosphere was good humored and the patrons were treated a little like school children. Léa addressed everyone informally, but no one was allowed to offer the slightest criticism of her establishment. If you found a speck of coal dust from the ancient range on your macaroni, that was just too bad.

In winter, when the weather was freezing cold and icy winds blew, the front door of the restaurant was closed. Customers had to go down a passage under the vaults and through Léa's kitchen. Some made it a regular habit. Even today, some of those who know of the second entrance prefer to use it. As a result, Philippe Rabatel has constructed a glass wall to the kitchen, in order to maintain hygiene.

Léa continued to supervise the kitchen until she finally retired at the age of 74. She moved to an apartment above the restaurant with views of the Rhône. Léa died in June, 1997, but her recipes are remembered. The current menu at *La Voûte* is faithful to her memory, listing such special treats as her delicious *bugnes*.

La Mère Castaing

On the other bank of the Rhône was another generation. At *Beau Rivage* a country inn in Coindrieu, Paulette Castaing was also called *mère* in recognition of her high-quality, simple cuisine that was in the style of the *mères* of Lyons. "You succeed only when doing something that you love," wrote the

Elegant, focused, and with an assured technique, Paulette Castaing tends the ranges at *Beau Rivage*.

French novelist Colette. The proof of this maxim is the fantastic success of the woman who declared, "I love cooking."

Born in 1911, the young Paulette Penel met Raymond Castaing while they were both apprentices at the Hotel Cheynet, in Alboussière in the Ardèche. Because of his ill-health, Raymond concentrated on restaurant service and management. He left Alboussière to train at the hotel management school in Nice. Paulette stayed behind, working as Mademoiselle Cheynet's sole assistant. Mademoiselle was an exceptional chef. "I had a real calling for cooking, and learned much from Mademoiselle Cheynet."

After marrying in 1933, the young couple initially worked in Megève, at Mademoiselle Rey's restaurants, *Les Fauvettes* and *Le Coq du Bruyère*. Later, during the dark years of World War II, they were employed at *Alaize*, a restaurant near Mère Brazier's on Rue Royale in

Lyons. Sometimes, Paulette Castaing smelled the aroma of fish emanating from the kitchen of the woman whom she called "Mère," but whose offer of work she had declined, finding her a little intimidating.

In 1946 Raymond and Paulette decided to set up their own business and found a charming old fisherman's cottage with a large, shady, terraced garden: the *Beau-Rivage* inn. It was a modest enterprise in the beginning. Madame Castaing commissioned a fish pond and she served freshly prepared trout *au bleu* (poached in a court bouillon) or *au champagne*. She also developed her own specialties: eel stew, the secret of which lay in poaching the eels in their skins so that the

flesh did not darken and deteriorate after skinning; and a pike mousseline which she made by pounding the fish by hand. "It was impressive to watch Madame Castaing working the paste with her spatula, with unbelievable force and skill," recalls Reynald Donet, the current chef at *Beau-Rivage*.

One day, the movie director Réné Clair and the actor Charles Vanel walked into the inn. Thanks to them, and especially thanks to Fernand Point, the chef of *La Pyramide* restaurant in Vienne, *Beau-Rivage* started to gain a reputation. Fernand Point, who was visited by all of the gourmets passing through southern France, praised Paulette's talents. Perhaps he sensed in her some of the spirit of his mother and grandmother who used to tend the ranges at the dining room of Louhans railroad station. He also persuaded the Castaings to upgrade their premises.

Beau-Rivage developed into a must-visit destination for lovers of fine food. Paulette Castaing was awarded her first Michelin star in 1954. A second one was awarded in 1964, and she kept both the stars until 1988, the year she sold the business to the Human-Donet family. They did their best to effect a smooth transition and, with this in view, the new chef, Reynald Donet, cooked alongside Paulette Castaing for six months. He remembers being impressed by the grand style of service at the restaurant which emulated that of aristocratic houses; waiters served from pedestal tables instead of bringing the food already on the plates.

Other Mères in France

At the beginning of the twentieth century, Mère Filloux was such a national celebrity that first-class female chefs in other regions of France also acquired the epithet of "*mère*."

La Mère Poulard

Time seems to stand still in the restaurant on Mont-Saint Michel. When you enter the kitchen, there is a chef beating a copper bowl full of dark yellow eggs, echoing the memory of Annette Poulard. Dexterously, he pours the foaming mixture into a pan of gently sizzling butter, holds the pan over the flame for a short while, takes it off, then returns it again, repeating the procedure until the omelet is fluffy and golden brown. He folds it in half, slides it onto a large plate, and sends it straight off to the waiting customer.

Annette Poulard in 1903: the inventive, avant-garde cook of Mont-Saint-Michel.

Today, as in times past, the omelet, the specialty of the house, is served all day long. Annette, who baked her bread fresh daily in a wood-fired oven, had the idea of cooking omelets for the visitors who arrived every day on *pataches*, a rickety form of public transportation, and were sometimes trapped on the hill by the weather and the tides. In the past there was no causeway and the fog could come into the bay and increase the chances of being caught in quicksand as you tried to cross to the mainland.

In May 1872 Annette Boutiaut first set foot on Mont-Saint-Michel. Born on April 15, 1851, in Nevers, she came from a poor family. She had come to the Mont with the Corroyer family who had employed her as a maid. Édouard Corroyer, an architect specializing in historic monuments, had just been commissioned to restore Mont-Saint-Michel

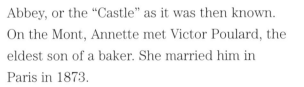

Abbey, or the "Castle" as it was then known. On the Mont, Annette met Victor Poulard, the eldest son of a baker. She married him in Paris in 1873.

When they returned to the Mont the young couple took over the running of the *Saint-Michel Teste d'Or* hostelry (the building now houses the post office). Then, they built the *Poulard Aîné* hostelry, which opened in 1888 with a sign proclaiming, *"A la renommée de l'omelette,"* home of the famous omelet.

Aside from knowing how to make the perfect omelet, Annette could bring out the best in all of the fine local produce of Brittany and Normandy: Eggs, butter, rich cream, extremely tender young lamb with a subtle iodine flavor from the salt-marshes, plump farmyard chickens, apples and fruits of the forest, potatoes and the various vegetables grown in the Armor region, wild Tombelaine mussels, fish (plaice, brill, turbot, sole, skate, and others), and berries. She also smoked salmon from the Sée, the Sélune, and Couesnon rivers at least twice a week.

Annette Poulard served the poor and the rich, including the British royal family, with equal pleasure. She delighted in running the

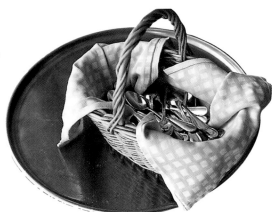

restaurant. Sometimes, she would accept a drawing or watercolor from an impoverished artist in lieu of payment.

Although Annette Poulard never moved from Mont-Saint-Michel, she was fully aware of the world through the numerous photographs and drawings sent to her from all corners of the globe by her customers. The walls of "l'Hermitage," the house to which she retired with her husband, were completely covered with the pictures. This gave Éric Vannier, the current proprietor, the idea of papering the restaurant's halls and dining room walls with 4,500 testimonials from Mère Poulard's guest book.

Annette was buried next to her husband in the tiny Mont-Saint-Michel cemetery on May 7, 1931, but her spirit lives on in her restaurant. A Norman arch that she had bought has been placed in front of the stone wall in the downstairs restaurant, and the dishes continue to be made with the best available local ingredients.

La Mère Blanc

The story of the Blanc family began the same year that Annette Boutiaut first set foot on Mont-Saint-Michel. In Vonnas, at the confluence of the Veyle and Renom rivers in the verdant heart of the Bresse region, Jean-Louis and his wife Virginie gave up farming and opened a country inn. Being close to the fairground where the poultry market was held, the restaurant attracted poulterers, gourmets, and others who appreciated its quality cooking. The restaurant's reputation spread rapidly.

Shortly after marrying Elisa Gervais, Adolphe Blanc took over the running of his parents' restaurant. Elisa, a passionate cook, brought with her many of her mother's recipes. These used generous quantities of butter and cream. She also had a repertoire of dishes learned during her apprenticeship with Madame Lambert-Peney, another chef in Vonnas.

Elisa Blanc's cuisine was based on the produce of Bresse—succulent golden colored chickens of unparalleled flavor; wonderful milk, cream, and butter; and fresh frogs, bought by the dozen from Dombes and transported to Vonnas in linen bags. Elisa's skill lay in selecting the best ingredients and cooking them perfectly. Her specialties,

The third generation of cooks in the Blanc family, Paulette, the author's mother, was an expert at controlling the temperature of her range.

Bresse chicken in a creamy sauce and little potato pancakes cooked in clarified butter, titillated her customers' palates. With the arrival of the automobile and extended railroad links, the inn's reputation spread far and wide. Entire families from Lyons and Mâcon traveled to Vonnas to eat at Mère Blanc's restaurant. In 1930, Elisa won the highest accolade in the first culinary competition sponsored by the Touring Club of France. The *Club des Cents* and the Academy of Gastronomes also honored her, while Curnonsky declared her "the best female cook in the world." The restaurant was awarded one Michelin star in 1931 and two the following year.

In 1934, Elisa began handing over the running of the restaurant to her eldest son, Jean, and his wife Paulette, formerly Tisserand, the daughter of the village baker. As Jean was not a cook, Paulette took charge of the kitchen. Elisa had an able pupil to whom she could pass on her recipes and her accomplishments.

For the next 34 years, Paulette Blanc continued to enhance the reputation of the inn by perfecting Mère Blanc's specialties and by offering her customers only the best Bresse produce, perfectly prepared.

Georges Blanc, a fitting heir to the Blanc family's culinary tradition, was born in 1943. From his early childhood, his grandmother introduced him to the pleasures of high-class comfort food, such as cakes in the shape of bananas that Elisa cooked on a small corrugated iron cookie sheet, and vanilla custards coated in caramel.

Having graduated top of his class from the school of hotel management at Thonon-les-Bains, Georges Blanc trained in Divonne-les-Bains and then in Beaulieu-sur-Mer. In 1965, he returned to Vonnas and learned from his mother Paulette how to prepare Elisa's superb recipes. Three years later, he took over the restaurant. Gradually, the country inn was transformed into one of the stars of the Relais and Château chain. The young chef

has since been showered with awards. In 1981, he was awarded three Michelin stars. In the same year, the Gault et Millau guide declared him "the chef of the year." Then in 1985, the same guide awarded him an exceptional 19.5 out of 20 points. He is a culinary star and people travel to the little village of Vonnas from around the world to sample his cooking.

Georges and Jacqueline Blanc's sons, Frédéric, born in 1966, and Alexandre, born in 1975, have both followed in the family tradition and trained as chefs. As the third millennium dawns, the future of the Blanc reputation seems secure.

Les Mères Allard

The Allard family culinary tradition does not extend quite so far back. Two generations of Allard women have been in charge of the kitchens of this famous Paris bistro: Marthe Allard, the founder, who has been described by Nicolas de Rabaudy, a food historian and writer, as a "Burgundian Mère Brazier," and her daughter-in-law, Fernande, to whom she has passed on her recipes and her skill in the kitchen.

One day, Marthe Meuriot, who was helping her mother at their café-tabac in Chailly-sur-Armançon (in the Morvan region), served a bacon omelet to Marcel Allard. However, history does not reveal whether the delicious omelet or the charm of the waitress seduced Marcel Allard into proposing!

Soon after marrying in 1920, the young couple moved to Paris and realized their

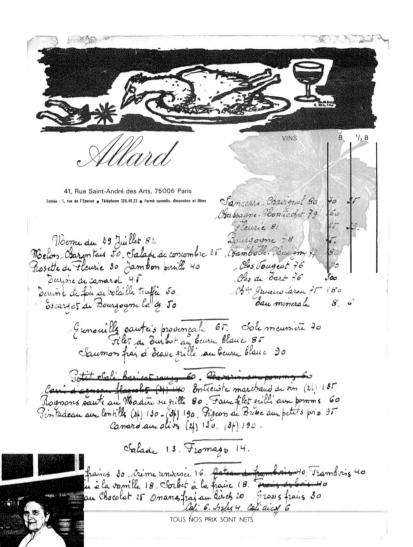

dream of owning a bistro in the 13th *arrondissement*. Marthe served generous portions of regional specialties to their mostly impoverished clientele. Her menu included dishes such as a hearty Burgundy stew, jugged rabbit, and pot-au-feu. One day a wine merchant told the couple about a bistro for sale in an ideal location in the 5th *arrondissement*. Vincent Candré was selling *À la halte de l'Éperon*, a restaurant known for its scallops in beurre blanc, chicken in red wine, and Chavignol wine. Marthe wrote a letter to her son André, who

Marthe Allard and her daughter-in-law Fernande: a successful example of the passing on of skills and recipes.

25

had been left behind in Burgundy, "The bistro is on Rue Saint-André-des-Arts. Your name. I hope that it will bring us good luck."

So began the Allard story. Marthe dedicated herself to cooking authentic Burgundian dishes, even mastering the famous beurre blanc whose secret Joséphine, Vincent Candré's cook, had confided to her. (Also known as white butter sauce, this is made from reduced vinegar and shallots to which butter is added.) She poured the sauce over pike poached in court-bouillon or, when in season, scallops. Marthe wrote the daily menu by hand. The food was, and still is, served on large oval platters, rather than on small plates. This allows for the generous presentation of a whole roast guinea fowl, lamb stew, chicken in red wine, lentils cooked with bacon, or a pheasant with chestnuts.

After World War II, André and his wife, Fernande, took over the bistro, whose reputation continued to grow. For the next 35 years, Fernande would prepare the same signature dishes: Cassoulet on Mondays, veal with onions and bacon on Tuesdays, lamb vegetable stew on Wednesdays, lentils with salt pork on Thursdays, braised beef with carrots on Fridays, and chicken in red wine on Saturdays.

Fernande, a native of Morvan like Marthe, not only captured André's heart, she also seduced her in-laws with her extraordinary *pâté en croûte* (pâté baked in a pastry crust). It was said that hers surpassed even that of renowned Chef Dumaine in Saulieu. Despite the arduous nature of the profession, the heavy pans and casseroles, and the unreliability of an ancient coal oven (always a worry when cooking soufflés), she happily took charge of the kitchen. Her strong personality, perseverance, and above all, perfectionism helped her to become a culinary star appreciated by gourmets the world over. "If your dish has no heart, it will be obvious; the food will not taste right. My cooking is based on simplicity, and that requires patience...," she explained to Nicolas de Rabaudy. She could have added: "and the very best ingredients available, chosen by André at the market."

André was expert at choosing produce and also at selecting wine. Every November, he and his father Marcel toured winemakers to make their purchases. They selected Beaujolais, Saint-Amour, Fleurie, Chirouble, Bonnes-Mares, and other very drinkable wines which paired well with the old-fashioned food that had all of Paris clamoring to eat at the bistro. The guest book is full of testimonials: "A source of love." (Jacques Brel); "Eat frequently with friends, at Allard and experience passion."(Peynet); "I want to sing 'Thank you, thank you, thank you.'" (Yvonne Printemps). People had to book eight days in advance to secure a table.

These days, there are three chefs in the kitchen. One of them, Didier Remay, was once Fernande's assistant. "She called us her

little cooks," he recalls. "Madame Fernande did not like working with women, she preferred supervising men. The first thing she told me was that I was to forget everything I might have learned elsewhere. We had to cook only her food. Madame Fernande watched us very closely. We were like a family

in the kitchen. Every August she treated us to a meal at a fine restaurant or a show at the Lido." Thanks to Didier Remay, the Allard tradition continues.

The current owner, Monsieur Layrac, is as particular about the quality of the produce used as were Marcel and André Allard in the past. He has added a few new dishes to the menu, including a succulent shoulder of lamb *baronet du Limousin*, which is, of course, served on a large, oval platter in the traditional Allard style.

Tarte aux cerises

**Tarte aux groseilles
à maquereau
vertes.**

Tarte Marinette.

Faites bouillir à f...
égoutter sur un tamis. Ra...
couche de sucre pilé au moment...

Prenez 350 grammes de farine, 325 gram...
3 jaunes d'œufs, 3 cuillerées de sucre, 2 cuille...
sur une plaque en trois parties ; une fois c...
une couche de confiture, couvrez de blancs d'...
mes de sucre, un jus de citron, faites cuire...

Dénoyautez les mirabelles, rangez-les...
...teur de la pâte sur le prem...
...vrez de sucre en...

La Mère Crouzier

Gisèle Crouzier was a native of Périgord. She "married her husband's profession" and, in 1945, found herself in the village of Chaumont-sur-Tharonne in the heart of the Sologne region as the chef of the hotel-restaurant *La Croix-Blanche*.

La Croix-Blanche is one of the oldest inns in France. It can trace its origins back to a simple inn that was on the same site in 1424—when Joan of Arc was fighting the enemy on the outskirts of Sologne. The restaurant is also unusual in its always having had female chefs. The first, Marie-Magdalene Thibonneau, began cooking in 1779. Since then, 18 women chefs have followed in her footsteps, providing fine food for connoisseurs.

Between 1945 and 1986, Gisèle Crouzier's delicious interpretations of traditional dishes from Sologne and Périgord gained *La Croix-Blanche* considerable fame. Today, Françoise Richard, a chef trained by Gisèle, still prepares those recipes. The specialties include: grand mique with veal kidneys and morels (miques are poached dumplings), duck or game terrines, wild duck surprise (the "surprise" is a fish stuffing), hare *à la royale* (braised and coated with a reduced cream sauce and truffles), and of course, the house specialty, created in 1969, rabbit Albicocco. This last recipe was named after the film director Jean-Gabriel Albicocco. Sologne was the romantically fog-shrouded setting for his movie Le *Grands Meaulnes* (*The Wanderer*). In the guest book he has written, "I have come back, after twenty-three years, to this happy house where, with a wonderful lady, I learned how to cook many delicious dishes and where, together, we created a recipe for rabbit with apricots that dear Madame Crouzier named after me."

To reach the dining room of this romantic inn, customers must go through the kitchen. It remains unchanged since the nineteenth century and one whole wall is taken up by a massive cabinet dating from 1850, which holds sparkling copper pans and jars of spices. "I liked to watch customers making their way through to the dining room while my apprentices and I tended the ranges. The apprentices were all girls aged 16 and 17. They were lively and neat, but most importantly, fond of their food. After watching me cook for six months, they mastered my recipes. Mostly, they remained with me until they were married."

Cooking? "It was not my profession, but Périgourdins all know how to cook. They watch their mothers and soon start cooking themselves. When I joined my husband, who had taken over *La Croix-Blanche* from his parents, my mother-in-law, Julia Crouzier, was in charge of the kitchen. My husband, who served as the maître d'hotel, carved poultry and game, and flambéed dishes at the table. He was also in charge of the wine service. More than anything else,

Gisèle Crouzier, helped by two of her female apprentices. As tradition dictates, only female chefs have worked at *La Croix-Blanche* since 1779.

I wanted to spend my life by his side. My mother-in-law, who was exhausted after years of hard work, taught me her recipes. I began to cook. After all, tradition at *La Croix-Blanche* dictated that women ran the kitchen. I think that I was so successful in Sologne because the flavor of my dishes could not be found elsewhere. When my mother made duck or goose *confit*, she collected the jelly that formed at the base of the pots and sent it to me in Chaumont. I used this extremely flavorful jelly as the base for my stocks. I devoted a lot of time to developing successful combinations of the fantastic produce available in Sologne."

The region is bursting with culinary riches. It includes some of the most extensive hunting grounds in France which are full of feathered and furred game (mallards, partridges, pheasants, hare, and wild rabbits, for example). The purple heath and red-leafed, silver-barked forest yields an array of wild mushrooms in the fall, such as firm, plump ceps (also known by their Italian name of *porcini* and their botanical name, boletus), the closely related red-capped pine or oak ceps, and crisp, dark yellow chanterelles (known in France as *girolles*). Gisèle Crouzier preserved 130 pounds of these mushrooms at a time. Sologne is also home to many freshwater lakes, bristling with downy reddish reeds, which yield carp, pike, eel, and pike perch or zander. Inspired, she created a sumptuous pike terrine *capucine*. She never actually tasted the food she was cooking; she knew instinctively when the seasoning was correct. She would, however,

have one of her apprentices taste it. Gisèle Crouzier cooked on an antique coal-fired range. When she needed a hotter burner, she would throw a handful of dry walnut shells and a few more pieces of coal onto the fire. Gisèle Crouzier, nicknamed "La Mère" by her clients from Lyons, was the guiding spirit of a peerless cuisine which had resulted from the melding of Périgord, her native region, and Sologne, her adopted home.

La Mère Adrienne

Regulars would comment affectionately, "La Vieille is not easy-going." La Vieille—the old woman—was the nickname of Adrienne Biasin, who cooked marvelous food in a pocket handkerchief-size restaurant in the heart of Paris between 1958 and 1993. From

a small village near Parme, Adrienne learned about good food by observing her mother from a very young age.

For a while, Adrienne worked as a waitress at a brasserie, an extremely taxing job. One of her customers teased her with the nickname "La Vieille." Clearly, she was not offended as she used it as the name of the

repertoire: Beef stew, braised beef with carrots, white veal ragout, and coq au vin. Jacques Manière and Raymond Oliver, great Parisian chefs of the period who bought their produce in the market daily, were attracted by the delicious aromas wafting from *Chez la Vieille*. They became regulars, sitting at a table at the back of the room with their cups

restaurant that she opened at the age of 25. In the beginning, she served only omelets and hearty snacks for the porters and agents who worked at *les Halles*, the Paris market, nearby. Some of her customers would even bring in their own piece of beef or slice of steak, which they would fry themselves on her range. This encouraged Adrienne to include a few more elaborate dishes in her

of coffee. Soon they also became Adrienne's friends and gave her invaluable advice on running her bistro. Through their influence, Adrienne was able to buy the best poultry and meat and the freshest vegetables at the lowest prices at *les Halles*.

One summer day, as the restaurant was empty, Adrienne decided to take a picnic to a friend's terrace in Montmartre. She was getting ready to pack the chickens that she had roasted when three customers arrived. Adrienne agreed to serve them, but only on condition that they accepted potluck. One of the customers, Philippe Couderc, was an influential food critic. He gave Adrienne's bistro pride of place in his column and her success was assured.

On the ground flour of a beautiful mansion at 37 Rue de l'Arbre-Sec, *Chez la Vieille* does not have a front entrance. Customers must go around the corner and push open the heavy door of 1 Rue de Bailleul. The prized address was guarded jealously by those in the know and tables had to be booked three months in advance at this restaurant with less than 30 covers and no printed menu. Adrienne or her sister, Madeleine, cheerfully recited the day's specialties.

Wearing her apron, Adrienne greeted her customers and seated them in the tiny room. A wide variety of appetizers covered the huge bar that took up at least a third of the room. These could include duck terrine, potted rabbit, headcheese (also known as brawn), *pâté de campagne*, salads, and Adrienne's famous stuffed tomatoes, warm from the oven.

Adrienne enjoyed cooking different dishes depending on how she felt or on the produce available in the market. However, after her Christmas menu was published by *Marie Claire* magazine in 1976, she was deluged for six months by new customers who all wanted to taste her scallops, leg of lamb, poached meringues, and chocolate cake. "They want only these dishes," she complained. "They do not understand that food must be different every day."

Her huge success, the relocation of *les Halles*, her two-year long series of programs on French television, "Adrienne at the table," the weekly column in *Madame Figaro* which she wrote for a year—none of these diminished Adrienne's authentic style. She turned down offers to move to larger premises or to set up a "grand" restaurant. She did not alter the size or the décor of her modest establishment, nor her personal, simple, and generous style of cooking. Her cuisine was

based on common sense and instinct, rather than fashion. Famous people, great chefs, and politicians all ate at her crowded tables. Her greatest thrill was when her idol, Jean Gabin, came to dine with his wife. Her greatest treat was being invited around the world to places such as Osaka and Dallas, or on cruises with great chefs, or to the Rio Carnival. A few years ago, Jean Tiberi, the mayor of Paris, invited her to cook a dinner for the 20 greatest Michelin-starred chefs in France. Without striving to impress, but cooking from the bottom of her heart, she served them *sole meunière* cooked with its skin on—"the dish is creamier and the delicate flesh of the sole is not harmed"—and a simple *navarin printanier*, a lamb stew with spring vegetables.

Doubtless she would still be cooking if she had not chosen to spend time with her husband, who has since died. *Chez la Vieille* still exists, but Gérard Besson and his assistant, Marie-José Cervoni, now run it.

La Mère Barale

Catarina-Elena Barale, a vivacious octogenarian known as Mère Barale, is an appropriate subject with whom to end this brief survey of France's tradition of *mères*. A journalist writing in *Nice-Matin* called her "the most delicious monument of Nice's culinary heritage."

The leading repository of traditional Niçois recipes, Mère Barale developed her culinary skills at *Chez Paulin et Ma* in the Riquier neighborhood. Her parents had been running the snack bar since 1916, the year of her birth. "Riquier was the most beautiful neighborhood in Nice. Before the 1940s, it

was like living in the countryside; there were meadows with cows and donkeys. I used to drink fresh warm milk."

Even at her age, she could still almost taste the authentic Nice specialties made by her mother Catarina, who in turn had learned how to cook them from her own mother. "Everything that I know about cooking, I was taught by my mother."

When she was 17, in 1933, Catarina-Elena Barale began running the snack bar, which by then had evolved into a restaurant. Fulfilling the promise of the restaurant's placard, *Catarina-Elena Barale, Especialita Nissarda, a la Bouana Franquetta*, for over 65 years, she has served her unique Niçoise specialties. These include *trouchia* or *troucha*, a bay-leaf scented omelet with cheese and *blea*, small-leafed Niçois chard; *tourta de blea*, a sweet pie filled with chard leaves, pine nuts, and raisins ("The best in Nice," according to connoisseurs);

Catarina-Elena Barale, Mère Barale, was declared "the most delicious monument of Nice's heritage," by the newspaper *Nice-Matin*.

pissaldiera, a pizza-like tart made by covering a bread dough base with a thick layer of onions which have been sweated in the local extra virgin olive oil. Mère Barale claims that "a good pissaladière ought to have a topping of onions that is at least as thick as the base. I always cry while peeling the tons of onions. I used to cook 14 pissaladières at a time in my clay oven. The oven dated from 1929, but after I converted it to gas, I continued to burn a few logs in a corner of it to flavor the food with the inimitable aroma of woodsmoke."

Estocaficada is another specialty, which has been popular in Nice for over 200 years. It is a highly seasoned, tomato-based stew made with dried haddock, *estocafic*—stockfish. Haddock used to be fished and dried in Norway before being traded in Nice for olive oil.

The *doba a la nissarda* is a rich beef stew, aromatically flavored with dried ceps and served with ravioli. Until recently, Mère Barale would make two thousand ravioli a day, by hand.

Finally, there is the *socca*, the snack favored both by locals and by the tourists who saunter across Saleya Square. A crisp, flat, corn-colored cake made from garbanzo bean flour, olive oil, and salted water, it is eaten hot off the griddle. "*Socca* must be cooked and eaten quickly because once cold, it is not good," insists Mère Barale. At her restaurant, *socca* are served after the pissaladière. Even Auguste Escoffier ate them at her restaurant!

In the evening, after the crunchy chard pie has been served for dessert, the pianola is started up. Everyone must then join Mère Barale in a spirited rendition, in Niçois, of "Viva, viva Nissa la Bella." "I would not consider retiring. When I am working, I am so busy that I don't even have the time to die!" exclaims Mère Barale.

The restaurant has walls made of rough-hewn stone and red and white drapes. It contains an amazing collection of bric-a-brac that would be the envy of most secondhand dealers. Enormous copper stills, old phonographs, scales, and kitchen equipment jostle for space with two 1925 Citröens. Catarina-Elena Barale is particularly attached to the two automobiles, as she passed her driving test in one of them in 1956. A hoarder, she has collected her whole life into her dining room. A celebrity in "Nissa la Bella," Mère Barale has always striven to make sure that at her restaurant the customers enjoy life while savoring the Niçois dishes that are so dear to her heart.

After a hectic meal service, sparkling clean glasses have been set out to dry on a damask cloth in a corner of the office.

Cooking with

the mothers

Crimini mushroom salad
with mussels

Salade de champignons de Paris aux moules was a part of the mixed hors d'oeuvres which Adrienne set out for her customers every day. Sometimes, she would also serve it as a vegetable accompaniment to slices of cold roast meat. Adrienne made it with the smallest, white crimini mushrooms, reminiscent of tiny, very pale portabello mushrooms. The dish always had a generous sprinkling of chopped fresh parsley "to dress it up!"

Serves 4

13½ cups/1 kg small, white crimini mushrooms

the juice of ½ lemon

2 tomatoes

3 shallots

3 tablespoons olive oil

1¼ cups/300 ml apple vinegar

1 lemon

1 garlic clove

2 tablespoons chopped fresh flat leaf parsley

4½ pounds/2 kg live mussels

salt and freshly ground pepper

Preparation time: 20 minutes
Cooking time: about 15 minutes

Trim the mushrooms. Rinse under cold running water and drain on paper towels. Sprinkle the mushrooms with the lemon juice and pat dry. If they are small, leave them whole. Quarter large ones.

Cut a small cross in the base of each tomato. Place them in a heatproof bowl and add boiling water to cover. After 10 seconds, drain well, peel, and seed.

Peel and finely chop the shallots. Heat the olive oil in a medium pan. Add the shallots and cook over low heat until they are translucent. Add the tomatoes, stir well, and cook for 3 minutes. Add the vinegar, then the mushrooms, and cover the pan.

Peel and thinly slice the lemon. Remove any seeds. Peel the garlic, cut it in half, and crush it with the flat side of a large knife.

Add the lemon slices, 1 tablespoon of the parsley, and the garlic to the pan. Season to taste with salt and pepper. Simmer gently for 10 minutes.

Meanwhile, scrub the mussels under cold running water and remove the beards. Discard any which do not close when sharply tapped. Put the mussels into a large, heavy pan with just the water clinging to their shells, cover, and cook over high heat, shaking the pan frequently, for 5 minutes, until the mussels have opened. Discard any that remain closed.

Transfer the mussels to a bowl using a slotted spoon. Strain the cooking liquid through a fine strainer into the pan of mushrooms. Reserve a few mussels for garnish and remove the remainder from their shells. Put all the mussels in a bowl.

Using a slotted spoon, transfer the mushrooms to the bowl. Return the pan to the heat, bring to a boil, and cook the liquid until slightly reduced. Pour it over the mushrooms and mussels, stir gently, and sprinkle with the remaining parsley. Serve hot or at room temperature.

La mère Adrienne

Adrienne's potted rabbit

Adrienne would make this delicious Rillettes de lapin façon Adrienne two or three days in advance. She added goose fat to the chopped rabbit to intensify the flavor. She served the potted rabbit in individual ramekins with thick slices of toast as a canapé.

Serves 6–8

1 calf's foot, split in half

7 medium onions

5 carrots

3 tablespoons olive oil

3 tablespoons peanut oil

14 ounces/400 g bacon or lightly salted pork side

4 pounds/1.8 kg rabbit portions

½ teaspoon coriander seeds

4 cups/1 liter white wine (preferably Muscadet)

1½ tablespoons white vermouth

1 bunch of fresh chervil

1 fresh tarragon sprig

scant 1 cup/200 g goose fat or shortening

salt and freshly ground pepper

To serve

crisp salad

toasted bread

mixed pickle (optional)

Preparation time: about 30 minutes

Cooking time: 3¼ hours

Put the calf's foot into a large pan, add cold water to cover, and bring to simmering point over low heat. Remove the calf's foot with a slotted spoon and rinse under cold water.

Peel and finely chop the onions. Peel the carrots and cut them into large pieces. Heat the olive and peanut oils in a large, heavy pan and cook the onions over low heat until softened, but not colored.

Place the pieces of calf's foot, bacon or pork, carrots, and rabbit portions on top of the onions. Season with salt and pepper and add the coriander seeds. Pour in the wine and vermouth, cover the pan, and simmer gently for 3 hours.

Remove the rabbit, bacon or pork, and calf's foot and let cool. Gently pull the meat from the rabbit portions and shred it.

Remove the bones from the calf's foot and finely chop the meat. Remove any rind from the bacon or pork and finely dice the meat. Strain the cooking liquid through a fine strainer and return it to the pan.

If necessary, boil the strained liquid until reduced to about 1¼ cups/300 ml. Put a few of the cooked carrots, the rabbit, chopped calf's foot, and bacon dice onto a large piece of clean cheesecloth. Using kitchen scissors, snip the chervil and tarragon over the top and tie the cheesecloth into a bag. Put the bag into the reduced liquid and simmer gently for 10 minutes.

Remove the cheesecloth bag. Add the goose fat or shortening to the pan and mix thoroughly. Tip the contents of the cheesecloth bag into an earthenware terrine and spread evenly with the back of a fork. Pour in a layer of melted goose fat or shortening. Decorate the top with a few pieces of cooked carrot. Let cool completely before covering with plastic wrap and chilling in the refrigerator.

Serve with a crisp salad and toasted crusty bread. Alternatively, it may be served with a mixed pickle of cornichons, onions, mushrooms, and Chinese artichokes.

La mère Adrienne

Scallops in beurre blanc

Regular customers declared Coquilles Saint-Jacques au beurre blanc, "The best scallops in the world." At the Allards' restaurant, scallops were on the menu only when in season. The season varied from year to year, but usually fell between October and May. Under the previous owner, Vincent Candré, the restaurant had become famous for its scallops "à la Vincent," in other words, scallops in beurre blanc. The recipe passed from Vincent's chef Joséphine to Marthe Allard virtually unchanged.

Rinse the scallops in cold water and remove the black intestinal tracts, if this has not already been done. Drain and gently pat dry on a dishtowel.

To make the beurre blanc, peel and finely chop the shallots. Place them in a heavy pan with the vinegar, sea salt, and peppercorns. Cook over low heat until the shallots are translucent and almost all the liquid has evaporated.

Cut the butter into small pieces and set it aside on a plate. Add a few pieces of butter to the shallots and whisk thoroughly until it is fully incorporated. Add the remaining butter, a few pieces at a time, making sure that each addition is fully incorporated before adding the next. Do not let the sauce boil.

Remove the pan from the heat and add the lemon juice. Strain through a fine strainer into the top of a double boiler or a heatproof bowl set over a pan of barely simmering water to keep it warm until you are ready to serve. Stir the beurre blanc occasionally to prevent it from separating. Do not let the base of the bowl touch the surface of the water.

Spread out a little flour on a plate or a sheet of baking parchment. Roll the scallops in the flour and shake off any excess: they need only a fine dusting.

Season the scallops with salt and pepper. Gently heat the butter and oil in a skillet. Cook the scallops for about 5 minutes, until they are a light golden color, turning frequently with a spatula.

Remove the skillet from the heat and transfer the scallops to a warmed serving dish. Pour a little of the beurre blanc over them. Pour the remaining sauce into a warmed sauceboat or pitcher. Serve the scallops immediately.

Serves 6

30–36 shelled fresh scallops
all-purpose flour, for dusting
¼ cup/50 g butter
2 tablespoons peanut oil
salt and freshly ground black pepper

For the beurre blanc

6 shallots
⅔ cup/150 ml white wine vinegar
½ teaspoon coarse sea salt
1 teaspoon crushed
white peppercorns
2½ cups/500 g chilled sweet butter
the juice of ½ lemon

Preparation time: 10 minutes
Cooking time: about 30 minutes

Les mères Allard

Parsleyed ham

Large and comforting, the generous slices of Jambon persillé served by Mère Allard overflowed the plate. Marthe Allard would make this meltingly tender and extremely flavorsome dish for both customers and staff. An easy recipe, it is ideal for serving to guests at an informal dinner party, as it can be made several days in advance.

Serves 8–10

2 carrots

2 onions

2 cloves

2 pieces of lightly salted ham on the bone, each weighing about 2¼ pounds/1 kg

1 calf's foot, split in half

1 bouquet garni

5 black peppercorns

8 shallots

4 garlic cloves

1 bunch of fresh flat leaf parsley

2 tablespoons strong Dijon mustard

2 tablespoons red wine vinegar

pinch of freshly grated nutmeg

pinch of 4-spice mixture (a mixture of ground pepper, grated nutmeg, ground cloves, and ground cinnamon)

salt and freshly ground pepper

cornichons and pickled onions, to serve

Preparation time: 30 minutes, the night before

Cooking time: 2½ hours

Chilling: 24 hours

The previous evening, peel the carrots and onions. Stick each onion with 1 clove. Slice the carrots.

Put the ham, calf's foot, onions, carrots, bouquet garni, and peppercorns in a large, flameproof casserole. Pour in enough cold water to cover and bring to a gentle simmer. Cook for 2½ hours, skimming off any scum that rises to the surface.

Meanwhile, peel and finely chop the shallots and garlic and place in a large bowl.

Remove and discard the stems of the parsley. Wash the parsley leaves and pat them dry on paper towels. Finely chop the leaves and stir into the shallots and garlic.

When the ham is cooked, remove the casserole from the heat and let cool.

Strain the stock into a bowl. Remove and finely chop the ham fat. Cut the meat off the bones and cut it into large cubes. Put the cubes into a terrine.

Add the fat to the bowl containing the shallots and garlic. Stir in the mustard and vinegar and season to taste with freshly grated nutmeg and 4-spice mixture. Add 4 ladles of the reserved stock and combine well. Taste and adjust the seasoning.

Pour the shallot mixture over the ham in the terrine and stir until thoroughly combined. Tap the terrine gently on the counter to level it and release any air bubbles. The surface of the terrine should be covered in liquid, so, if necessary, add some more of the stock. Cover the dish with plastic wrap and chill in the refrigerator for 24 hours.

Serve the terrine, cut into slices, with cornichons and pickled onions.

Les mères Allard

Niçoise Salad

According to Mère Barale, this is the authentic way to prepare Salada nissarda. She made her salad using only locally grown, fresh vegetables. As a snack, she served "lou pan bagnat"—the Niçoise salad mixture stuffed into a crusty bread roll that has been split in half and liberally doused with olive oil.

Wash and dry the tomatoes, radishes, and green bell peppers. Shell the baby fava beans. Cut off the bases of the scallions and remove the outer layers. Slice the tomatoes. Spread the tomato slices out on a large plate and sprinkle them with salt.

Cook the eggs in boiling water for 12 minutes. Drain and immediately run them under cold water.

Trim the stems of the artichokes and remove the outer leaves. Cut the artichokes into small pieces and immediately sprinkle them with olive oil and a few drops of vinegar to prevent them from discoloring.

Drain the oil from the tuna and the anchovy fillets. Flake the tuna with a fork.

Pour off any liquid released by the tomatoes and arrange the slices, overlapping slightly, on a large serving dish. Slice the radishes thinly. Sprinkle them over the tomatoes. Season with salt and pepper.

Cut each bell pepper in half and remove the seeds. Thinly slice the bell peppers and the scallions and sprinkle them over the tomatoes. Add the artichoke pieces. Shell the eggs, cut them into rounds, and add to the dish. Season with salt and pepper. Top the salad with the flaked tuna, anchovy fillets, baby fava beans, and olives.

Chill the salad. Just before serving, drizzle some olive oil and a few drops of vinegar over the salad. Serve cold.

Serves 6

10 tomatoes

1 bunch of radishes

4 small, green bell peppers

9 ounces/250 g baby fava beans in their shells

2 bunches of scallions

4 eggs

5 baby globe artichokes

1 tablespoon extra virgin olive oil, plus extra for drizzling

red wine vinegar, for drizzling

11 oz/300 g canned tuna in olive oil

12 canned anchovy fillets in oil

1¼ cups/150 g black olives, preferably Niçoise

salt and freshly ground pepper

Preparation time: 20 minutes
Cooking time: 12 minutes

La mère Barale

Pissaladière

The pissaladière derives its name from pissalat ("peis sala," salted fish), a Provençal condiment which is made from a purée of sardines and anchovies blended with olive oil and delicately flavored with cloves, wild thyme, and bay leaves. This specialty is something of a local secret. It is often replaced by anchovy fillets canned in olive oil. Here is a version for the home kitchen.

2 pissaladières serving

8 people each

For the dough

1 cup/250 ml lukewarm water

1½ tablespoons salt

¾ ounce/20 g fresh yeast

9 cups/1 kg all-purpose flour

7 tablespoons olive oil, plus extra
for brushing

2 eggs

For the topping

10 pounds/4.5 kg onions

1½ cups/350 ml olive oil

1 bouquet garni (parsley sprigs,
rosemary, thyme, bay leaf)

about 30 small Niçoise olives, pitted

3 tomatoes

12 canned anchovy fillets, drained or
12 salted anchovy fillets, rinsed

salt and freshly ground black pepper

Preparation time: 40 minutes

Cooking time:
about 1 hour 20 minutes

Rising: 1½ hours

To make the dough, divide the water between 2 small bowls. Dissolve the salt in 1 bowl and the yeast in the other. Sift the flour onto a large wooden board or a counter. Make a well in the center and pour in the olive oil, salted water, and eggs. Gently combine the ingredients. Add the dissolved yeast. Knead the dough for at least 10 minutes, until it is smooth and elastic. Form the dough into a ball, place it in a bowl, and cover with a dishtowel. Set aside in a warm, draft-free place for at least 1 hour, until it has doubled in bulk.

Meanwhile, peel and finely chop the onions. Heat the olive oil over medium heat in a heavy, flameproof casserole. Gently stir in the onions and the bouquet garni, cover, and cook over very low heat for about 30 minutes, until the onions are translucent, but not caramelized. Season the onions with salt and pepper.

Divide the dough in half. Brush 2 large cookie sheets with oil. Using your hands, shape each ball of dough into a 10-inch/ 25-cm round, about ⅝ inch/1.5 cm thick. With the help of a rolling pin, transfer the rounds onto the prepared cookie sheets. Crimp the edges, cover the dough with a dishtowel, and let rest for about 30 minutes.

Remove and discard the bouquet garni from the casserole. Spread the onions in an even layer on both the dough rounds. Cover 1 pissaladière with olives. Slice the tomatoes and spread them on the other. Top with the anchovies arranged like the spokes of a bicycle wheel and any remaining olives.

Cook the pissaladières in a preheated oven, 425°F/220°C/gas mark 7, for about 30 minutes.

Slide the cooked pissaladières onto cooling racks and grind black pepper over them. Serve them hot or warm.

La mère Barale

Chicken liver pâté

Mère Blanc only ever used the pale yellow livers of Bresse chickens for her Pâté de foies blonds. These have absolutely no hint of bitterness. For an authentic flavor, if Bresse chicken livers are not available, order the livers of free-range, grain-fed chickens from your butcher.

Serves 6–8

1½ pounds/700 g fatty pork
½ onion
1 garlic clove
1½ cups/40 g parsley leaves
5 tablespoons Madeira
2 tablespoons vegetable oil
pinch of freshly grated nutmeg
14 ounces/400 g chicken livers
1 large sheet of thin pork fat back
or 6–8 fatty bacon strips
1 envelope Madeira aspic
salt and freshly ground black pepper
salad, to serve

Preparation time: 15 minutes,
2 days before serving;
45 minutes the day before
Marinating: 12 hours
Chilling: 24 hours
Cooking time:
2 hours and 40 minutes

The night before, cut the pork into small pieces. Peel and quarter the onion. Peel the garlic. Wash and dry the parsley leaves. Put the pork into a large bowl with the onion, garlic, and parsley. Pour in the Madeira and stir to coat. Cover the bowl and let marinate overnight in the refrigerator.

The next day, remove the pork from the marinade, reserving the vegetables. Heat the oil in a skillet over high heat and cook the pork pieces, stirring frequently, for about 10 minutes. Season with salt, pepper, and grated nutmeg. Let cool and then chill.

Trim the chicken livers and remove any veins or green spots. Combine the livers, pork, and reserved vegetables. Work the mixture through the medium blade of a meat grinder. (If you do not have a grinder, you can use a food processor: First pulse the marinade vegetables, then add the pork, and pulse a few times. Finally, add the livers and pulse just once or twice.)

Line the base and sides of a terrine with the fat back or bacon, leaving enough overhanging the edges to cover the top later. Spoon the liver mixture into the terrine, packing it down firmly. Bring the fat back or bacon over the top. Place the terrine in a bain marie or roasting pan half-filled with hot water and cook in a preheated oven, 300°F/150°C/gas mark 2, for 2½ hours. If necessary, add more hot water to the bain marie or roasting pan.

Remove the terrine from the oven and let cool to room temperature. Then, chill in the refrigerator for 24 hours.

Prepare the Madeira aspic according to the packet instructions. Pour it over the terrine and chill until set.

Serve the terrine in slices with a salad.

La mère Blanc

Chicken and duck liver mousse with truffles

Mousse de foies de volaille truffée is a rich and flavorsome appetizer. The truffles can be replaced with peeled pistachios or finely chopped truffle parings. For an unusual presentation, make balls of the mousse (after it has been chilled overnight) and roll them in finely chopped truffles or pistachios. Keep them in the refrigerator until just before serving.

The night before, trim the chicken livers duck livers, if using, and remove any veins or green spots.

Make up 1 cup/250 ml of the aspic according to the packet instructions. Chill in the refrigerator.

Melt the butter in a heavy skillet and cook the livers over low heat for 5 minutes. Do not let them brown or they will dry out. Season to taste with salt and freshly ground pepper. Using a slotted spoon, transfer the livers to a food processor.

Pour off the fat from the skillet and return it to high heat. Pour in the port and brandy and stir well, scraping any sediment from the base of skillet. Bring the mixture to a boil, then strain, and add to the livers. Process, add the pieces of foie gras, and process again. Add the crème fraîche and half of the aspic. Process to a smooth and even mousse. Using a rubber spatula, scrape the mixture into a cheesecloth-lined strainer and push it through. Taste and adjust the seasoning, if necessary.

Finely chop the truffles and stir them into the mousse. Transfer the mixture to a terrine and smooth the top. Cover with a thin layer of the prepared aspic. Pour any remaining aspic into a soup plate. Chill the mousse and the aspic for at least 24 hours.

Serve the mousse with toasted slices of country bread and cubes of aspic.

Serves 6

8 Bresse chicken livers or 4 duck livers and 4 chicken livers
1 envelope aspic powder
1½ tablespoons/20 g sweet butter
1 tablespoon port
1 tablespoon brandy
5 ounces/150 g duck or goose foie gras or foie gras mousse
⅔ cup/150 ml crème fraîche
¾ ounce/20 g truffles or truffle parings
salt and freshly ground pepper
toasted country bread, to serve

Preparation time:
30 minutes, the night before
Chilling: 24 hours
Cooking time: 5 minutes

La mère Blanc

Country-style terrine

Paulette Blanc would make this extremely tasty Terrine campagnarde several days in advance so that the flavors had time to mature. The foie gras in the recipe gives the terrine a particularly velvety texture. Paulette served it simply, with just cornichons and homemade pickled onions.

Ask your butcher to bone the duck and, in addition to the meat, ask for the carcass, neck, and liver. Remove the skin and any tendons or veins from the duck meat. Cut the duck, veal, pork, and fat into ¼-inch/ 5-mm strips. Put the strips into a large bowl, season with salt, pepper, and 4-spice powder, and drizzle with the brandy, port, and truffle juice, if using. Mix well, cover with plastic wrap, and chill for 6 hours.

Peel and dice the carrot, shallot, onion, and celery. Chop the duck carcass and neck into pieces. Melt 6 tablespoons of the butter in a flameproof casserole over medium heat. Brown the duck carcass and neck with the vegetables for about 5 minutes. Season, add the bouquet garni and water, and cover. Lower the heat and simmer for 30 minutes. Pour the stock through a fine strainer.

Make the aspic according to the packet instructions. Stir in the stock.

Melt the remaining butter in a skillet over medium heat. Cook all the livers for 2 minutes on each side, until just pink. Season with salt and pepper.

Remove the strips of duck breast meat from the marinade. Work the remaining meat through the medium blade of a meat grinder.(If you do not have a grinder, put the meat in a food processor and pulse 2–3 times until roughly chopped.) Chop all of the livers, together with the foie gras. Using a wooden spoon, thoroughly combine the meats and the livers with the marinade. If you like, add some chopped truffle.

Line the base and sides of a terrine with the sheets of fat back or bacon strips, leaving enough overhanging the sides to cover the top later. Spoon in a layer of the liver mixture. Cover with half the reserved strips of duck. Make another layer of liver mixture and top with the remaining duck. Finish with a final layer of liver mixture, smooth the top. and fold over the overhanging fat back or bacon to enclose.

Place the terrine in a bain marie or roasting pan half-filled with hot water and cook in a preheated oven, 350°F/180°C/gas mark 4, for 2 hours. Add more hot water during cooking, if necessary.

Remove the terrine from the oven. Place a board just inside the dish or cut a piece of card to the right size, wrap in baking parchment, and place it on top of the terrine. Put a weight, such as 2 cans of tomatoes, on top and set aside in a cool place for about 2 hours.

Pour any juices released by the terrine into a pan, add the aspic, and bring to a boil. Lower the heat and simmer for about 10 minutes. Skim off any fat.

Top the terrine with a ladle of aspic. Wait a moment before adding a second ladle. Continue in this way until there is a ½-inch/ 1 cm layer of liquid on top of the terrine. Cover and chill for 2–3 days. Pour any remaining aspic into a bowl and chill.

Remove the terrine from the refrigerator at least 2 hours before serving. Serve in slices with aspic cubes and a salad.

Serves 12

1 × 6½ pound/3 kg Barbary duck
11 ounces/300 g veal rump
11 ounces/300 g lean pork shoulder
14 ounces/400 g fresh pork fat
pinch of 4-spice mixture (a mixture of ground pepper, grated nutmeg, ground cloves, and ground cinnamon)
½ teaspoon brandy
¼ cup/50 ml port
3 tablespoons truffle juice (optional)
1 large carrot
1 shallot
1 onion
½ celery stalk
7 tablespoons/100 g sweet butter
1 bouquet garni
1¼ cups/300 ml water
1 envelope aspic
10 chicken livers
3½ ounces/100 g foie gras or foie gras mousse
1 truffle (optional)
4 thin sheets of pork fat back or
10–12 fatty bacon strips
salt and freshly ground black pepper
salad, to serve

Preparation time:
3 days in advance, 1 hour
Marinating: 6 hours
Resting: 2 hours
Cooking time: about 2¼ hours
Chilling: 3 days

La mère Blanc

Mère Bourgeois'
warm pâté

The international reputation of Mère Bourgeois' cooking at the beginning of the twentieth century owed much to Le pâté chaud de la mère Bourgeois. The Aga Khan, King Umberto of Italy, chief justice and mayor of Lyons, Édouard Herriot, and famous figures of the age all made their way to the tiny village of Priay to sample her extraordinary warm pâté.

Serves 8–10

1 × 4 pound/1.8 kg chicken, with giblets

2 carrots

4 shallots

1 tablespoon/15 g sweet butter

5 ounces/150 g pork shoulder

5 ounces/150 g veal rump

5 ounces/150 g fatty pork or fresh pork fat

3 fresh parsley sprigs

12 black peppercorns

scant 1 cup/200 ml Madeira

1 raw duck foie gras weighing about 1¼ pounds/550 g

2 ounces/50 g truffles or truffle parings

1 tablespoon/15 g sweet butter, plus extra for greasing

7 tablespoons Madeira

2 eggs

1 thin sheet pork fat back or 6 fatty bacon strips

salt and freshly ground black pepper

(continued on page 56)

The day before serving, ask your butcher to skin and bone the chicken. Use the carcass to make the chicken stock.

Peel and slice the carrots and shallots. Melt the butter in a skillet over medium heat. Cook the sliced vegetables for a few minutes, then transfer them to a large bowl.

Remove any tendons from the chicken thigh meat. Cut the thigh meat, pork shoulder, veal, and fatty pork or pork fat into large cubes. Slice the chicken breast fillets into thin strips. Put all of the meat, with the parsley and peppercorns into the bowl with the vegetables. Stir in the Madeira and 4 cups/1 liter of the cooled chicken stock. Cover and marinate overnight in the refrigerator.

Meanwhile, make the pastry. Sift the flour into a bowl and make a well in the center. Dice the butter and add it to the well with the salt. Add the eggs and knead rapidly, adding a few drops of water to make a dough. Form the dough into a ball, cover with plastic wrap, and chill overnight.

Next day, remove the dough from the refrigerator. Soften the foie gras by soaking it in lukewarm water, then pull the 2 lobes apart using your hands. Pat dry. Place the lobes, inside out, on a cutting board and gently cut away any veins. Season with salt and pepper.

Chop the truffles and work them into the foie gras, along with any truffle preserving juice. Form the lobes into a sausage shape. Cover and chill.

Remove the meat from the marinade. Set aside the strips of chicken. Pile the remaining meat on a cutting board and season with salt and pepper.

Melt the butter and briefly cook the chicken liver until it is just pink. Add it to the pile of mixed meat and, using a sharp knife, finely chop the the mixture. Transfer to a bowl, add the Madeira and the eggs, and mix well.

Lightly grease a *pâté en croûte* mold or meat loaf pan. Roll out three-quarters of the dough into a rectangle. Use the rolling pin to lift the dough and place it in the mold or pan. Leaving a narrow edge, trim off any excess dough.

Line the dough with the sheets of fat back or bacon strips, leaving an overhang and pressing it into the corners.

La mère Bourgeois

For the pastry

5 cups/500 g all-purpose flour

1½ cups/350 g softened sweet butter

pinch of salt

2 eggs

1 egg yolk, for glazing

Preparation time:

the day before, 20 minutes

on the day, 30 minutes

Marinating: 12 hours

Cooking time: about 1½ hours

Spoon half of the meat mixture into the mold or pan. Place half of the chicken strips on top and gently press them into the meat mixture. Place the foie gras on top and cover it with the remaining meat mixture. Embed the rest of the chicken strips as before. Fold over the fat back or bacon to enclose and trim any excess.

Roll out the remaining dough into a rectangle. Using a pastry brush, dampen the edge of the dough in the mold and place the lid on top. Crimp the edges with your fingers. Using a sharp knife, make a pattern on the lid and cut 3 holes, each about ½ inch/1 cm in diameter. Brush the dough with beaten egg yolk.

Cut 3 small rectangles out of card. Roll them up and put these "chimneys" into the holes. Place the mold on a cookie sheet and bake in a preheated oven, 475°F/240°C/gas mark 9, for 15 minutes. Reduce the oven temperature to 350°F/180°C/gas mark 4 and bake for 1¼ hours more. Check the pâté once or twice and cover it with a piece of foil if the pastry looks like it might burn.

Remove the pâté from the oven, carefully remove the "chimneys," and let it rest at room temperature for at least 20 minutes before attempting to remove it from the mold. However, you should not let it rest for too long; Mère Bourgeois' pâté should be served warm.

La mère Bourgeois

Vegetarian stuffed tomatoes

Mère Bourgeois made this simple dish of Tomates au maigre using the juiciest tomatoes and fresh herbs from the kitchen garden at Priay. If you cannot find fresh Belgian endive, it can be replaced with a few sorrel leaves.

Wash and dry the tomatoes. Cut a small "lid" off the top of each and reserve. Using a teaspoon, scoop out the seeds. Put a pinch of sugar into each tomato.

Put the tomatoes into a greased, shallow ovenproof dish. Bake in a preheated oven, 400°F/200°C/gas mark 6, for 15 minutes. Transfer the tomatoes to a cutting board to drain off any excess juice.

Cook the eggs in boiling water for 12 minutes. Drain and cool them under cold running water. Crush the stale bread into crumbs with a rolling pin or in a food processor. Wash and dry the parsley leaves and Belgian endive and chop them finely.

Peel the garlic, cut it in half, then crush the halves using the side of a large knife.

Shell and halve the eggs. Put them in a bowl and mash coarsely with a fork. Add the stale bread crumbs, parsley, Belgian endive, garlic, and crème fraîche. Season to taste with salt and freshly ground black pepper and mix well.

Fill the tomatoes with the egg mixture and return them to the ovenproof dish. Cover each tomato with a "lid." Sprinkle them with the dried bread crumbs and dot with the butter.

Bake in a preheated oven, 350°F/180°C/gas mark 4, for 45 minutes, basting the tomatoes frequently.

Serve the tomatoes straight from the oven as an appetizer or as a vegetable accompaniment to broiled steak.

Serves 6

6 large, ripe tomatoes

1 tablespoon superfine sugar

2 tablespoons/25 g sweet butter, plus extra for greasing

2 eggs

7 ounces/200 g stale bread, about 7 thick slices

3½ cups/100 g fresh flat leaf parsley

3½ ounces/100 g Belgian endive

1 garlic clove

scant 1 cup/200 ml thick crème fraîche

dried bread crumbs, for sprinkling

salt and freshly ground black pepper

Preparation time: 15 minutes

Cooking time: about 1 hour

La mère Bourgeois

Onion soup gratinée

Mère Brazier would use the stock produced when she cooked poached chickens to make delicious white sauces, enriched with tapioca, crème fraîche, egg yolks, and, quite often, strips of fresh truffles. She would also use it as the base for this wonderful Gratinée lyonnaise.

Serves 6

7 ounces/200 g onions

1 tablespoon/15 g sweet butter

8¾ cups/2 liters chicken stock

1 day-old baguette

1¾ cups/200 g grated Swiss cheese, plus extra to serve

3 egg yolks

⅔ cup/150 ml port

freshly ground black pepper

Preparation time: 10 minutes

Cooking time: about 45 minutes

Peel and finely chop the onions. Melt the butter over low heat in a heavy, flameproof casserole. Add the onions and cook, stirring frequently, for 10 minutes, or until they are golden. Add the chicken stock. Bring the soup to a gentle boil and simmer for about 10 minutes.

Slice the baguette into fairly thick rounds. Place the rounds on a cookie sheet and bake in a preheated oven, 350°F/180°C/gas mark 4, until the croûtons are crisp and lightly colored.

Put a layer of croûtons in the base of an ovenproof tureen and sprinkle with a thin layer of grated Swiss cheese. Alternate the layers until all the croûtons and cheese have been used, finishing with a layer of grated Swiss cheese.

Carefully ladle the soup over the croûtons. Put the tureen on the lowest shelf of the oven and cook for about 30 minutes.

In a small bowl, whisk the egg yolks and port with a fork. Season to taste with pepper.

As soon as the topping is golden brown, remove the tureen from the oven. Push aside the crust and take out a ladle of soup. Carefully pour this into the egg yolk mixture, whisking constantly. Pour the egg yolk mixture back into the tureen, under the crust, and stir carefully to combine with the rest of the liquid. Serve immediately, passing around an additional bowl of grated Swiss cheese.

La mère Brazier

Terrine of the house

Each mère had her own terrine recipe. This Terrine maison is packed with flavor, even when made without truffles. It is the perfect, reliable appetizer when entertaining, especially as it is made at least two days ahead of time.

Serves 8–10

1¼ pounds/500 g veal rump, in 2 pieces

1¼ pounds/500 g pork shoulder

1 rindless unsmoked ham hock

10 chicken livers

pinch of freshly grated nutmeg

3 cups/750 ml dry white wine

¼ cup/50 ml brandy

2 eggs

scant 2 cups/100 g fresh bread crumbs

1 truffle

3½ oz/100 g cooked foie gras

2 thin sheets of fat back large enough to line the terrine or 10–12 fatty bacon strips

rendered pork fat or clarified butter

salt and freshly ground black pepper

To serve

cornichons

crisp salad

toasted country bread

Preparation time: the day before, 20 minutes; on the day, 20 minutes

Marinating: 24 hours

Cooking time: about 3 hours

Chilling: 2 days

The day before, cut half of the veal rump into thin slices. Cut the other half into large cubes. Cut the pork shoulder into cubes. Cut the meat off the hock and then into cubes. Work the cubed meat and the chicken livers through a meat grinder. Alternatively, pulse the mixture briefly in a food processor—it should be in fairly large pieces, not puréed.

Put the ground meat and the veal slices into a large bowl. Season to taste with salt, pepper and freshly grated nutmeg. Pour in the white wine and brandy and mix well. Cover with plastic wrap and marinate in the refrigerator for 24 hours.

Next day, remove the veal slices from the marinade. Cut them into ½-inch/1-cm wide strips.

Break the eggs into the bowl of ground meat. Break up any clumps in the bread crumbs and add them to the bowl. Stir until the ingredients are thoroughly combined.

Thinly slice the truffle. Form the foie gras into a sausage shape the same length as your terrine.

Line the terrine with a sheet of fat back or bacon strips. Spoon in a layer of the ground meat mixture, pressing it down firmly. Place half the veal strips on top. Make another layer of ground meat mixture. Place the foie gras "sausage" on top and cover it with the truffle slices. Add another layer of ground meat mixture, followed by the remaining veal strips. Finish with a final layer of ground meat. Cover the terrine with a sheet of fat back of bacon strips, tucking the edges down the inside of the terrine.

Put the terrine into a large, ovenproof dish or roasting pan. Pour in boiling water to come two-thirds of the way up the side of the terrine. Cook in a preheated oven, 275°F/140°C/gas mark 1, for about 3 hours. Add more water to the dish or roasting pan during cooking, if necessary.

Remove the terrine from the dish or pan and let cool completely. Spread the top with a thin layer of rendered pork fat or clarified butter. Chill the terrine for at least 2 days before serving it with cornichons, a crisp salad, and slices of toasted country bread.

La mère Brazier

Spiny lobster Belle-Aurore

Spiny lobster, like this Langouste Belle-Aurore, was very fashionable in the 1920s. It featured on Mère Brazier's first ever menu. For the price of five French francs, she served a daring menu of spiny lobster in mayonnaise, pigeon with peas and carrots, and brioche with apples flambéed in rum.

Peel and finely dice the carrot, shallots, and celery. Heat the butter in a large sauté pan and add the vegetables with the thyme and bay leaf. Cover the pan and cook over low heat, stirring occasionally, for about 20 minutes, until the vegetables are softened and translucent.

On a cutting board with a channel to collect any liquid, split the lobsters' heads from the thoraxes. Remove the stomach sac from behind the head of each lobster.

Put the bodies and heads into the sauté pan with any liquid that has collected on the cutting board. Cook, stirring, for a few minutes. Add the brandy and set it alight. When the flames have died down, half-fill the pan with water. Season with a little salt, ground pepper, and a tiny pinch of cayenne. Cover and simmer for about 20 minutes.

Remove the lobster pieces from the pan. Bring the cooking liquid to a boil over a medium heat and boil until reduced by half.

Meanwhile, cut the shells off the lobsters using a pair of kitchen scissors. Slice the tail sections into medallions and place them on a warmed serving platter.

Remove all of the meat from the heads of the lobsters and add it to the reduced cooking liquid. Cover the pan and reheat the sauce, stirring occasionally.

Strain the sauce through a fine strainer into a clean pan. Stir in the crème fraîche and tomato paste and cook over a medium heat until the sauce is thick enough to coat the back of a wooden spoon. Taste and adjust the seasoning, if necessary. Bring the sauce to a boil and pour it over the lobster medallions. Serve immediately.

Serves 4

1 carrot

2 shallots

1 celery stalk

1½ tablespoons/20 g sweet butter

1 fresh thyme sprig

1 bay leaf

2 live spiny lobsters weighing about 2¼ pounds/1 kg each

¼ cup/50 ml brandy

pinch of cayenne pepper

2¼ cups/500 ml crème fraîche

¼ teaspoon tomato paste

salt and freshly ground pepper

Preparation time: 25 minutes

Cooking time: about 45 minutes

La mère Brazier

Artichoke hearts with foie gras

Fonds d'artichaut au foie gras was one of Mère Brazier's great specialties. She adopted Mère Filloux's recipe, but preferred to serve the foie gras on cold artichoke hearts. She felt that serving the artichoke hearts warm caused the foie gras to deteriorate, spoiling the dish.

Serves 6

juice of 1 lemon

6 large globe artichokes

mixed salad greens

6 slices of cooked duck foie gras, chilled

coarse sea salt

warm toast, to serve

For the vinaigrette

1 small onion

½ teaspoon chopped fresh flat leaf parsley

½ teaspoon chopped fresh tarragon

½ teaspoon chopped fresh chervil

3 tablespoons red wine vinegar

9 tablespoons extra virgin olive oil

salt and freshly ground pepper

Preparation time: 15 minutes

Cooking time: about 20 minutes

Pour the lemon juice into a large bowl of cold water.

Wedge the head of 1 globe artichoke on the corner of a table and break off the stem: the fibrous part should come away cleanly. Trim the base of the artichoke. Remove the outer leaves until you reach the little purple leaves. With a sharp knife cut off the cone of purple leaves. Drop the trimmed artichoke into the acidulated water to prevent it from discoloring. Repeat the process with all the remaining artichokes.

Drain the artichokes and put them into a large pan. Cover with cold water, add sea salt, and bring to a boil over low heat. Tuck baking parchment into the pan so that the hearts are not exposed to the air. Simmer for 20–25 minutes, depending on the size of the artichokes. Check to see if they are cooked by piercing the hearts with the point of a knife or a fork.

Drain the artichokes and dry them with a dishtowel. Carefully remove the chokes using a small teaspoon. Set aside and cover with a dishtowel.

To make the vinaigrette, peel and finely chop the onion. Put it into a bowl with the parsley, tarragon, and chervil. Add the vinegar and oil. Season with salt and freshly ground pepper and whisk until combined.

Add the artichokes to the vinaigrette and marinate for 15 minutes.

Wash and dry the salad greens. Toss with a little of the vinaigrette and arrange on a serving dish. Place the artichoke hearts on top and top each of them with a well-chilled slice of foie gras. Serve immediately with warm toast.

La mère Brazier

Dandelion leaf salad

Léa would buy her dandelion leaves from the Quai Saint-Antoine market near her restaurant, which sold a wide variety of baby salad greens. Gathered in meadows in spring, wild dandelion leaves are known in Lyons as "groin d'âne"—donkey muzzles. Make this Salade aux pissenlits sauvages on the day you pick the leaves, as they wilt very quickly.

Put the smoked herring in a shallow, ovenproof dish. Bake in a preheated oven, 475°F/240°C/gas mark 9, until the skin begins to blister. Remove the herring from the oven and let cool.

Skin the herring and carefully remove all the bones. Mash the flesh with 1 tablespoon of the white wine vinegar.

Snap or cut off the roots and wash the dandelion leaves several times in cold water mixed with the remaining vinegar. Dry the leaves and chill them.

Cook the eggs in boiling salted water for 10 minutes.

Meanwhile, combine all the vinaigrette ingredients, whisking well.

Heat the oil in a skillet and fry the bread until it is golden on both sides. Drain the fried bread on paper towels and cover with more paper towels. Press gently to remove the excess oil.

Put the smoked herring purée into a salad bowl and stir in vinaigrette to taste.

Peel and halve the garlic clove and rub the cut sides on the fried bread. Cut the bread into small croûtons.

Shell the hard-cooked eggs. Chop 4 of them into small pieces and cut the rest in half lengthwise.

Toss the dandelion leaves with the small pieces of egg, croûtons, and herring sauce. Garnish with the halved eggs and serve.

Serves 4

1 smoked herring fillet

2 tablespoons white wine vinegar

1¾ pounds/800g wild dandelion leaves

8 eggs

2 tablespoons vegetable oil

4 slices of day-old country bread

1 garlic clove

For the vinaigrette

5 tablespoons peanut oil

2 tablespoons red wine vinegar

salt and freshly ground pepper

Preparation time: 20 minutes

Cooking time: about 35 minutes

La mère Léa

Appetizers

65

Chilled mackerel in white wine

Léa's refreshing and delicious Maquereaux glacés au vin blanc requires a young, slightly dry, white wine. Mackerel are at their best from the beginning of May through the end of September. They have larger reserves of oil at this time, making their flesh tender and full of flavor. You could prepare young mackerel in the same manner, allowing two fish per person.

The day before, ask your fish store to gut the mackerel through the gills. Wipe the mackerel inside and out with damp paper towels. Do not wash them—washing would strip the fish of the oils that give them flavor and a supple texture.

Pour the water into a pan. Add the clove, coriander, and fennel seeds. Bring to a boil over medium heat, then remove the pan from the heat. Cover and let the spices steep for 20 minutes.

Peel the onions. Cut them in half and slice thinly.

Arrange the mackerel, head to tail, in a single layer in a sauté pan. Season with salt and pepper. Strain the marinade onto the fish. Add the white wine and the onion slices. Bring to a boil over low heat and simmer for 5 minutes. Remove the pan from the heat, cover, and let cool.

Carefully transfer the contents of the pan to a shallow bowl, cover, and chill in the refrigerator until the next day.

Next day, lift the mackerel out of the marinade. Fillet it, removing any small bones with tweezers and all of the skin. Put the fillets on a serving dish and sprinkle with the sliced onions and pieces of jellied marinade. Chill until ready to serve, as the dish tastes best when thoroughly cold. Wash and dry the chervil. Pick the leaves off the stems.

To serve, drizzle the mackerel with the white wine vinegar and garnish with the chervil leaves.

Serves 4

4 very fresh mackerel
2¼ cups/500 ml water
1 clove
½ teaspoon ground coriander
1 teaspoon ground fennel seeds
2 onions
⅔ cup/150 ml. white wine
1 tablespoon white wine vinegar
5 fresh chervil sprigs, to garnish
salt and freshly ground pepper

Preparation time: 30 minutes
Chilling: 24 hours
Cooking time: about 10 minutes

La mère Léa

Cockle and mussel soup

Mère Poulard would cook Soupe de moules et de coques de la Baie with the wild mussels and cockles brought by the basketful by egg-sellers returning from Tombelaine beach. They took care to rinse the shellfish in seawater before delivering them to Mont Saint-Michel. Mère Poulard always served an extra platter of cockles and mussels with this specialty of the region.

The previous day, put the cockles in a large bowl of cold water. Add a whole egg, in its shell, and stir in coarse sea salt. When the egg bobs to the surface of the water, the salinity is equivalent to that of seawater. Add the cockles and let stand overnight. The cockles will then slowly cleanse themselves of any sand they hold inside. It is not necessary to do this with clams.

Next day, scrub the mussels and clams, if using, under cold running water and remove the beards. Discard any that do not close when sharply tapped. Put them into a bowl of cold water and stir. Strain both the cockles or clams and the mussels.

Peel and chop the shallot. Put it into a large pan with the white wine. Bring to a boil over high heat and add the shellfish. Cover and cook for about 5 minutes, until the shells have opened. Line a colander with cheesecloth and strain the shellfish, reserving the cooking liquid.

Melt half of the butter in a flameproof casserole over low heat. Stir in the flour and cook, stirring constantly, for about 1 minute. Add the fish stock and the reserved cooking liquid and simmer gently until the mixture begins to bubble. Whisk in the crème fraîche and the remaining butter. Season with salt and freshly ground pepper to taste and add the shellfish.

Reheat the soup, then pour it into a tureen. Chop the parsley, sprinkle it on the soup, and serve immediately.

Serves 4

4½ pounds/2 kg live cockles or clams
1 egg
coarse sea salt
3¼ pounds/1.5 kg live mussels
1 shallot
7 tablespoons dry white wine
¼ cup/50 g butter
¼ cup/25 g all-purpose flour
4 cups/1 liter fish stock (see page122)
⅔ cup/150 ml crème fraîche
½ bunch fresh parsley
salt and freshly ground pepper

Preparation time: 20 minutes
Soaking: 12 hours
Cooking time: about 15 minutes

La mère Poulard

LE MONT SAINT-MICHEL. — *Pêcheurs des Grèves et Coquetières.* — LL.

Samphire salad with marinated sea bass and salmon

Samphire grows in the crevices of rocks or on cliffs by the seashore. It is known by a variety of regional nicknames: "perce-pierre," rock-borer; "casse-pierre," cliff-breaker; "pousse-pierre," rock-mover. Often, the fleshy leaves, which are a rich source of iodine, are pickled in vinegar. Fresh samphire is best for this Salade de cristes-marines aux bar et saumon marinés.

Serves 4

1 sea bass fillet, weighing
11 ounces/300 g
1 salmon fillet, weighing
3½ ounces/100 g
3 cups/400 g fresh samphire
or pickled if fresh is not available
(there is no real substitute, but this
dish could be made with young
asparagus or green beans)
juice of 1 lemon
¼ cup/50 ml sherry vinegar
7 tablespoons vegetable oil
2 shallots
1 bunch of fresh chives
½ bunch of fresh chervil
salt and freshly ground black pepper

Preparation time: 20 minutes
Cooking time: 5 minutes

Using a very sharp knife and cutting on the diagonal, slice the sea bass fillet and the salmon into very thin strips. Divide the fish among individual plates, cover with plastic wrap, and chill.

Wash the samphire thoroughly in cold water. Plunge it into a pan of boiling, lightly salted, water. Bring back to a boil and blanch for 2 minutes. Drain, then refresh the samphire in a large bowl full of ice cubes. Drain and pat dry with paper towels. Put it in a bowl.

Combine the lemon juice and vinegar. Gradually whisk in the oil. Peel and finely chop the shallots and add them to the vinaigrette. Mix well and season with salt and freshly ground pepper.

Toss the samphire in a little of the vinaigrette. Chop the chives and add to the remaining vinaigrette. Pour this over the strips of sea bass and salmon. Add some samphire to each plate, grind black pepper over the salad, and garnish with sprigs of chervil. Serve immediately.

La mère Poulard

Veal kidneys
"à la perle"

Rognon de veau "à la perle" was the favorite of Adrienne's good friend and customer, Lino Ventura. A wizard at the stove, Adrienne would test the kidneys to see if they were ready by pressing them gently with her fingers. A perfectly cooked kidney, when cut, will ooze a juice that forms beads (like a pearl), hence the expression "à la perle."

Serves 2

1 fresh veal kidney,
fat and membrane removed

½ teaspoon vegetable oil

pinch of dried thyme

1 bay leaf

2 tablespoons/30 g sweet butter

5 tablespoons thick
crème fraîche

2 tablespoons chopped
fresh flat leaf parsley

salt and freshly ground pepper

Preparation time: 5 minutes

Cooking time: about 25 minutes

Remove any remaining fat from the outside of the kidney.

Brush a small sauté pan or a heavy skillet with the oil, then heat. (The pan should be just large enough to hold the kidney.) Gently brown the kidney on all sides over low heat. Add the thyme and bay leaf and season to taste with salt and pepper. Add a pat of the butter and the crème fraiche. Cook for about 15 minutes over low heat, turning the kidney several times so that it cooks evenly and is well coated in the sauce. Transfer the kidney to a warmed serving dish, cover, and keep warm.

Remove the pan from the heat, and vigorously whisk the remaining butter into the pan juices. Pour the sauce over the kidney, sprinkle with chopped parsley, and serve immediately. Adrienne would serve this dish with spinach.

La mère Adrienne

Roast pork with kidney bean purée

A grand, crispy roast to serve in the fall or winter with the year's new crop of dried kidney beans. Sometimes, Adrienne would also serve Palette de porc rôtie à la purée de haricots rouges with potato, chestnut, or celery root purée. This recipe will be most successful if made from high-quality pork.

Put the kidney beans in a bowl, cover with cold water, and soak for 2 hours.

Drain the beans and put them in a large pan. Cover with cold water and add the bouquet garni and the large onion. Bring to a boil and boil vigorously for 15 minutes. Lower the heat to medium and cook for about 1½ hours. Season with coarse salt when the beans are nearly tender.

Meanwhile, peel the carrots, pearl onions, shallots, and garlic. Quarter the onions, shallots, and carrots and thinly slice the garlic. Insert the garlic slivers between the fat and flesh of the pork. Melt the pork fat or shortening and brush it over the pork.

Put the pork into a roasting pan large enough to hold it and the vegetables. Roast in a preheated oven, 400°F/200°C/gas mark 6, until well browned. Reduce the oven temperature to 350°F/180°C/gas mark 4 and cook for about 1 hour, basting frequently with a little of the bean cooking liquid.

Finely chop the sage leaves and sprinkle them onto the cooked pork. Baste the pork with some of the roasting juices. Let the roast rest in the oven, with the heat turned off, while you make the purée.

Drain the beans, reserving a little of the cooking liquid and discarding the bouquet garni. Pass the beans through a food mill, adding a little of the cooking liquid to help make a purée. When the purée has reached the right consistency (neither too liquid, nor too dry) add the butter and beat until it is fully incorporated. Season to taste.

Place the roast on a large platter. Pour off any excess fat from the roasting pan. Add the water to the pan and bring it to a boil on the stovetop, stirring constantly and scraping up any caramelized sediment from the base of the pan. Strain the deglazing juices through a fine strainer into a sauceboat. Serve the roast with the warm *jus* and the kidney bean purée.

Serves 6

generous 3 cups/500 g dried kidney beans

1 bouquet garni

1 large onion stuck with 1 clove

3 carrots

5 pearl onions

2 shallots

2 garlic cloves

1 pork blade shoulder, boned, weighing 3¼ pounds/1.5 kg

4 tablespoons rendered pork fat or shortening

1 fresh sage sprig

3 tablespoons/40 g sweet butter

⅔ cup/150 ml water

coarse salt, salt and freshly ground pepper

Preparation time: 10 minutes
Soaking: 2 hours
Cooking time: about 1½ hours

La mère Adrienne

Beef with carrots

On the days when she had Boeuf aux carottes on the menu, Adrienne would rise at 5 o'clock in the morning. The quality of this dish, which helped to confirm Adrienne's reputation, depends upon long, slow cooking in a cast iron casserole. Adrienne claimed that it was "a dish for all seasons. My customers would enjoy it both in summer and in winter." On warm days, she would serve it cold with lots of carrots and crisp salad greens.

Serves 6

½ teaspoon vegetable oil

4 pounds/1.8 kg beef brisket

1 calf's foot, split in half

1 veal knuckle, cracked

1 oxtail, cut in pieces

2 onions

4 leeks

1 bouquet garni

2¼ cups/500 ml dry white wine

5½ pounds/2.5 kg carrots

3 tablespoons chopped fresh flat leaf parsley

salt and freshly ground pepper

Preparation time: 20 minutes

Cooking time: about 4½ hours

Put the oil in a large Dutch oven or heavy flameproof casserole. Add the brisket, fat side down, and cook until well browned. Turn it over and add the calf's foot, veal knuckle, and oxtail.

Cook over low heat for about 10 minutes, stirring frequently. Remove all the meat and pour away the fat. Wipe the casserole with a paper towel and return the meat to it.

Peel the onions and cut each into 6 pieces. Wash the leeks, cut off and discard the green parts, and slice the white parts. Add the onions, leeks, and bouquet garni to the casserole. Season with salt and pepper. Add the white wine and sufficient water to cover the contents of the casserole by about ½ inch/1 cm. Cover and simmer for 3 hours.

Meanwhile, peel and thickly slice the carrots. Add them to the casserole, cover, and simmer for at least 1 hour more.

Remove all the meat from the casserole. Discard the veal knuckle. Let the brisket rest for at least 10 minutes before cutting it in slices. Cut the meat from the calf's foot and cut it into small pieces. Arrange the slices of beef, the oxtail, and the cubes of calf's foot on a warmed serving dish. Surround the meat with the carrots.

Return the casserole to the heat and bring to a boil. Remove and discard the bouquet garni.

Ladle the cooking juices over the meat. Sprinkle chopped parsley over the dish and serve very hot.

La mère Adrienne

Country casserole

The secret of Adrienne's extraordinary Pot-au-feu campagnard lies in soaking the meat in cold water overnight before cooking it with a packet of the vegetable parings (apart from potato peel) wrapped in a piece of cheesecloth. She would use any leftover meat to make stuffed tomatoes for the following day.

The day before serving, rub the ribs, beef shank, and veal shin with coarse sea salt. Put the meat in a large, nonmetallic bowl, add cold water to cover, and chill overnight.

Next day, rinse the salted meat under cold running water and pat dry. Put the ribs and beef shank into a large stockpot or flameproof casserole. Cover with cold water. Add the onion, bouquet garni, and celery. Bring to a boil over low heat, skimming off any scum that rises to the surface.

Peel the carrots, turnips, and celery root. Wash the leeks and cut off the green parts. Put the vegetable peelings and the green part of the leeks into a piece of cheesecloth. Tie the cheesecloth into a bag. Roll the celery root in the lemon juice to prevent it from discoloring.

When no more scum is rising to the surface of the stockpot, add the cheesecloth bag. Cover and simmer for about 2½ hours. Add the ham knuckle and the veal shin and cook for 1 hour more.

Using kitchen string, tie the white parts of the leeks in 2 bundles. Quarter the celery root and roll the pieces in lemon juice. Peel the potatoes. Put the carrots, turnips, and the celery root into a large pan and cover with cold water. Bring to a boil over low heat and cook for 15 minutes. Add the potatoes and the leek bundles. Season sparingly with salt and cook for about 40 minutes more. Drain the vegetables and keep warm.

Put the marrow in a pan and cover with cold water. Bring to a boil over low heat. Skim off any scum that rises to the surface and poach gently for about 20 minutes.

Discard the cheesecloth bag and bouquet garni, transfer the meat from the stockpot to large plates, and keep warm. Pour the stock into a warmed tureen. Toast the slices of bread. Serve the soup with the toast, adding a slice of marrow bone and some coarse sea salt to each piece.

Slice the meat and place it on a large, warmed, serving dish. Surround the meat with the vegetables.

Garnish with chopped parsley and serve with little bowls of coarse salt, crushed black peppercorns, cornichons, and a variety of mustards.

Serves 12

3¼ pounds/1.5 kg beef short ribs
4½ pounds/2 kg beef shank
1 veal shin
1½ cups/250 g coarse sea salt
1 onion stuck with 1 clove
1 bouquet garni
1 celery stalk
15 carrots
15 small turnips
1 celery root
15 leeks
juice of ½ lemon
1 fresh ham, knuckle end
15 potatoes, roughly the same size
12 slices of bone marrow
12 slices of rustic bread
4 tablespoons chopped fresh parsley
salt and freshly ground pepper

To serve

coarse sea salt
crushed black peppercorns
cornichons
mustard

Preparation time:
5 minutes the day before;
30 minutes on the day
Soaking: 12 hours
Cooking time: about 4 hours

La mère Adrienne

Stuffed tomatoes

Adrienne suggested "making the filling for Tomates farcies in advance so that the flavors have time to intermingle." Depending on her mood, she would cook the tomatoes on a bed of rice or just with some butter in the pan. When there was not enough leftover cooked meat in the kitchen, she would add some good quality sausage meat and some stale bread soaked in a little milk.

Serves 6

1 medium slice of baked, dry-cured or lightly smoked ham

about 11 ounces/300 g leftover meat from Country casserole (see page 77) or cold roast pork

1 bunch of fresh mixed fresh herbs, such as flat leaf parsley, chives, and chervil

4 shallots

1 garlic clove

scant ½ cup/100 g sweet butter

1 extra large egg

pinch of 4-spice mixture (a mixture of ground pepper, grated nutmeg, ground cloves, and ground cinnamon)

6 large tomatoes

1 cup/75 g freshly grated Parmesan cheese

6 tablespoons red rice, such as Wehani or Carmargue

1¼ cups/300 ml stock from Country casserole (see page 77) or beef stock

salt and freshly ground pepper

Preparation time: 20 minutes

Cooking time: about 1 hour

Remove and discard the rind from the ham. Cut off and reserve any fat. Chop the cooked meat, ham, and ham fat. Wash, dry, and finely chop the herbs. Combine them with the chopped meat.

Peel and finely chop the shallots. Peel the garlic and crush it with the flat blade of a large knife. Melt 1 tablespoon/15 g of the butter in a skillet. Add the garlic and shallots and cook over low heat until softened, but not colored. Pour off any excess fat. Stir the garlic and shallots into the chopped meat mixture with the egg. Season to taste with salt, pepper, and 4-spice mixture.

Wash and dry the tomatoes. Cut a "lid" off each and reserve. With a teaspoon, scoop out the flesh, leaving a ¼-inch/5-mm thick shell. Coarsely chop the tomato flesh and

set aside in a bowl. At the last minute, mix the tomato pulp and the grated Parmesan with the rest of the filling.

Lightly sprinkle the inside of the tomato shells with salt. Stand them upside down on paper towels to drain off any excess juice.

Stir the tomato flesh and Parmesan into the meat mixture, then fill the tomato shells with the stuffing. Top them with the "lids."

Generously grease a shallow ovenproof dish with butter and spoon in the rice. Place the tomatoes on top of the rice and dot each tomato with butter. Spoon a little stock over the tomatoes.

Bake in a preheated oven, 425°F/220°C/gas mark 7, for 40 minutes. From time to time, while the tomatoes are baking, pour the remaining stock over them. Serve the stuffed tomatoes straight from the dish.

La mère Adrienne

Veal riblets with lemon

"I love veal riblets because they are crunchy and succulent. I won a competition organized by a brand of aperitif with this recipe." Depending on what was available at the market, Adrienne would accompany Tendrons de veau au citron with celery or leeks, or perhaps with a pasta dish—macaroni mixed with diced tomatoes, grated carrot, and zucchini, coated with crème fraîche mixed with chopped parsley and chervil.

Trim the scallions, but leave them whole. Peel the shallot.

Heat the butter and oil in a large, heavy pan over medium heat. Add the riblets and cook, turning occasionally, until they have browned on both sides. Add the bouquet garni, scallions, and shallot. Roughly chop the tomatoes and add them to the pan. Season to taste with salt and pepper. Simmer for 15 minutes over low heat.

Meanwhile, wash the leeks and cut off and discard the green parts. Cut the white parts in half lengthwise, then cut them into 2½-inch/6-cm thick slices. Transfer the riblets to a plate and keep warm.

Add the leeks and white wine to the pan. Bring to a boil, then reduce the heat, and simmer for 15 minutes.

Return the riblets to the pan, placing them on top of the leeks. Add any meat juices they may have released onto the plate. Cover and simmer over very low heat for 15 minutes. Add the crème fraîche and cook until the liquid in the casserole has reduced and thickened.

Arrange the leeks and scallions in a bed on a serving platter. Top with the veal riblets and sprinkle with chopped parsley. Place a slice of lemon on each riblet and serve immediately.

Serves 4

15 scallions
1 shallot
¼ cup/50 g sweet butter
2 tablespoons vegetable oil
1¼ pounds/500 g breast of veal cut into 4 riblets or chops (if you can buy Parisian-cut veal, look for *tendrons*)
1 bouquet garni
3 large tomatoes
8 leeks
2¼ cups/500 ml dry white wine
1 cup/250 ml crème fraîche
3 tablespoons chopped fresh parsley
1 lemon
salt and freshly ground pepper

Preparation time: 25 minutes
Cooking time: about 50 minutes

La mère Adrienne

Chicken in red wine

Coq au vin was the most popular dish served at Marthe Allard's restaurant. The flesh of a rooster can be tough, so the bird has to be cooked slowly, for a long time. Both to reduce her costs and to increase the flavor of the dish, Marthe Allard would use the fat in the cavity of the bird to cook it. The sauce is traditionally thickened with blood, but you could use beurre manié—made by blending 4 tablespoons flour and 2 tablespoons softened butter—whisked in, small pieces at a time, at the last minute.

Serves 8

1 × 5¼ pound/2.4 kg chicken, cut into 8 pieces

2 tablespoons fat from the chicken or vegetable oil

3 tablespoons all-purpose flour

7 ounces/200 g fatty bacon, about 7 thick strips or 14 thin strips

2 onions

3 garlic cloves

1 tablespoon tomato paste

1 bouquet garni

⅔ cup/150 ml brandy

8 cups/2 liters red wine

2¾ cups/200 g crimini mushrooms

2 tablespoons chicken or pork blood (optional)

salt and freshly ground pepper

steamed parsley potatoes, to serve

Preparation time: 25 minutes
Cooking time: about 3½ hours

Collect about 2 tablespoons of fat from the cavity of the chicken and cut it into small pieces. Melt the fat or if you like heat the vegetable oil in a large skillet over high heat. Spread out the flour on a plate and roll the pieces of chicken in it, shaking off any excess. Add to the skillet and cook, turning frequently, until browned on all sides.

Remove the chicken from the skillet with a slotted spoon and transfer it to a flameproof casserole set over low heat.

Cut the bacon into small dice. Return the skillet to the heat, add the bacon, and cook until browned. Transfer to the casserole with a slotted spoon.

Peel and chop the onions. Add them to the skillet and cook over low heat, stirring occasionally, until translucent. Transfer to the casserole with a slotted spoon

Peel and finely chop the garlic. Add to the casserole with the tomato paste and bouquet garni. Stir in the brandy and set it

alight. When the flames have died down, add the red wine. Bring to a boil and set it alight. Season with salt and pepper. Lower the heat, cover, and simmer for 2–3 hours, depending on the age of the chicken.

Cut off the mushroom stems, wash the caps, and pat dry. Slice the caps and add them to the casserole. Cook for a few minutes more.

When the chicken pieces are tender, transfer them to a serving dish, using a slotted spoon. Keep warm.

Increase the heat under the casserole and boil the cooking liquid until it is reduced and lightly coats the back of a wooden spoon. Take out a ladle of sauce and mix it into the blood, if using. Pour the mixture back into the casserole, whisking vigorously. Remove and discard the bouquet garni. Spoon the sauce over the chicken pieces and serve immediately with steamed parsley potatoes.

Les mères Allard

Guinea fowl with lentils

Guinea fowl, known as the "painted bird" in France, has a fine and delicate flavor reminiscent of pheasant, so lentils make a good partner. Marthe Allard would cook her lentils in a chicken stock flavored with bacon. In France, only green Puy lentils have been accorded "appellation d'origine contrôlée" status. They are very small with slight blue markings. The larger red lentils have a much softer texture that is less suitable for Pintade aux lentilles.

Cut the bacon into small dice with a sharp knife. Heat 2 tablespoons of the shortening or oil in a flameproof casserole. Add the bacon and fry until the fat runs.

Peel and finely chop 2 of the onions. Add them to the bacon and cook over medium heat, stirring occasionally, until translucent. Reserve ⅔ cup/150 ml of the white stock and add the remainder to the casserole with 1 of the bouquets garnis. Season with salt and pepper and simmer for 1½ hours.

Heat the remaining shortening or oil in a Dutch oven or oval casserole over medium heat. Add the guinea fowl and cook, turning frequently, until browned all over. Add the butter. Cover, lower the heat, and cook for 40 minutes, turning frequently.

Put the lentils in a large pan. Peel and quarter the remaining onions. Add to the lentils with the remaining bouquet garni.

Add cold water to cover. Bring to a boil and simmer for 25 minutes over low heat.

Remove the guinea fowl from the casserole, set aside, and keep warm. Pour off any fat from the casserole and return it to the heat. Stir in the reserved white stock, scraping up any sediment from the base of the casserole. Cook until reduced and slightly thickened.

Cut the guinea fowl into serving pieces, put them on a platter, and spoon some of the gravy over them. Pour the remaining gravy into a sauceboat.

Strain the lentils, season to taste with salt, and stir them into the bacon and stock mixture. Remove and discard the bouquets garnis and the pieces of onion. Bring to a boil and cook for 2 minutes, then transfer to a deep serving dish. Serve the lentils with the guinea fowl and gravy.

Serves 4

5 ounces/150 g fatty bacon, about 5 thick strips or 10 thin strips

3 tablespoons shortening or vegetable oil

4 onions

4 cups/1 liter white stock (see page 84)

2 bouquets garnis

1 × 3½ pound/1.6 kg guinea fowl

2 tablespoons/30 g butter

2½ cups/500 g Puy lentils

salt and freshly ground pepper

Preparation time: 20 minutes

Cooking time: about 1¾ hours

Les mères Allard

Lamb stew
with potatoes

Navarin d'agneau aux pommes de terre was a classic of first Marthe and later, Fernande Allard's kitchen. The success of this easy-to-make, delicious, and meltingly tender stew depends on the quality of the meat and long, slow cooking. Marthe's special variation was to brown the lamb in hot goose fat. This would impart a strong, nutty flavor to the meat.

Serves 8

2 tablespoons goose fat or vegetable oil

5½ pounds/2.5 kg boneless stewing lamb, trimmed and cubed

3 onions

3 tablespoons all-purpose flour

4 cups/1 liter dry white wine

2 garlic cloves

1 bouquet garni

2 tablespoons tomato paste

3¼ pounds/1.5 kg waxy potatoes

⅔ cup/150 ml water

1 tablespoon chopped fresh flat leaf parsley

salt and freshly ground pepper

For the white stock (makes 4 cups/1 liter)

2¼ pounds/1 kg cracked veal bones or chicken giblets

8 cups/2 liters water

2 carrots

1 large onion

1 clove

2 celery stalks

1 leek, white part only

2 garlic cloves

1 bouquet garni

salt and white peppercorns

Preparation time:
20 minutes the day before;
25 minutes on the day

Cooking time:
3 hours the day before,
1 hour on the day

Make the white stock the day before you plan to cook the stew. Put the veal bones or giblets in a stockpot with the water. Bring to a boil over medium heat, skimming off any scum that rises to the surface.

Peel the carrots and onion. Quarter the onion and stick the clove into 1 piece. Cut the other vegetables into pieces. Peel and chop the garlic. Add the vegetables and garlic to the pot with the bouquet garni and a few peppercorns. Season with salt.

Bring the stock back to a boil, then lower the heat to a gentle simmer. Cover and simmer for 3 hours.

Remove the stockpot from the heat, let cool completely, then chill overnight.

Next day, remove the layer of fat that will have set on top of the stock. Strain the stock through a cheesecloth lined strainer into a bowl.

Heat half the goose fat or oil in a skillet over high heat. Add the lamb, in batches, and cook, stirring frequently, until browned all over. Transfer to a flameproof casserole and set over a low heat.

Peel and finely chop the onions. Add them to the skillet and cook, stirring

occasionally, until golden, then transfer to the casserole. Sprinkle the flour into the casserole and mix well. Cook, stirring constantly, over medium heat until the flour begins to change color. Stir in the wine and half the white stock.

Peel the garlic cloves. Add them to the casserole with the bouquet garni and the tomato paste. Season with salt and pepper. Mix well, cover, and simmer for 45 minutes.

Meanwhile, peel the potatoes and cut them into large pieces. Put the potatoes, the remaining stock and goose fat or oil, and the water into a casserole. Cover and cook for 25 minutes, until tender when pierced with the point of a sharp knife.

When the lamb is cooked, transfer it to a warmed, deep dish with a slotted spoon and keep warm.

Return the casserole to the heat and boil until the liquid is reduced and just thick enough to coat the back of a spoon. Pour the sauce through a fine strainer over the lamb. Put the potatoes in another serving dish and spoon some of their cooking liquid over them. Sprinkle parsley on the potatoes. Serve immediately.

Les mères Allard

Duck with olives

Canard aux olives is only as good as the ingredients. The olives should be both fleshy and crunchy, such as the unpitted, brine-cured, large green olives from Gard or Corsica and Lucques olives from the Languedoc. The stock must be homemade and the duck should, of course, be of the highest quality. The Allards would serve the duck on a bed of olives and carve at the table, but at home, it easier to serve ready carved.

Serves 4

9 cups/1 kg green olives cured in brine

2 large onions

4 chicken necks

5 chicken wings

5 chicken gizzards

2 tablespoons duck fat or vegetable oil

3 tablespoons all-purpose flour

¼ cup/50 ml dry white wine

13 cups/3 liters white stock (see page 84)

1 bouquet garni

scant 1 cup/200 g tomato paste

1 × 4½ pound/2 kg oven-ready duck (the Allards used Nantais duck, but this is now difficult to obtain, even in France)

2 tablespoons/30 g butter

salt and freshly ground black pepper

Preparation time:
30 minutes the day before;
20 minutes on the day
Cooking time: about 4 hours

The day before serving, pit the olives and put them in a bowl of cold water. Leave them to soak overnight.

Next day, peel and slice the onions. Chop the chicken necks, wings, and gizzards into small pieces. Heat the duck fat or oil in a flameproof casserole over high heat, add the chicken pieces, and cook, stirring frequently, until browned all over. Add the onions and cook until translucent. Sprinkle the flour into the casserole and cook for a few minutes. Add the wine and 8 cups/ 2 liters of the stock. Add the bouquet garni and the tomato paste and season with salt and pepper. Stir well and bring to a boil.

Cover the casserole and transfer it to a preheated oven, 300°F/150°C/gas mark 2, and cook for about 4 hours, checking occasionally that it has not dried out.

Drain the olives. Put them into a pan and add the remaining stock. Simmer for 2 hours over very gentle heat.

Remove the casserole from the oven and strain the stock into the olive pan. Simmer for a further 2 hours.

Place the duck on its side in a roasting pan. Roast in a preheated oven, 475°F/ 240°C/gas mark 9, for 15 minutes, until browned. Lower the temperature to 400°F/ 200°C/gas mark 6, add the butter, and turn the duck onto its other side. Cook for 30 minutes more, basting frequently, and occasionally sprinkling with some of the olive stock.

Transfer the duck to a carving board. Pour off any fat from the roasting pan, but reserve the juices. Add the olives and their stock to the roasting pan and stir well.

Carve the duck breast into strips. Cut off the legs. Pour any meat juices from the carving board over the olives. Put the pieces of duck on a deep serving dish. Cover them with the olives and spoon the sauce over them. Serve immediately.

Les mères Allard

Salade
Crème glacée à la vanille 18
Charlotte au Chocolat 25

Veal with onions and bacon

Veau à la berrichonne—Berry is an old French province—is a nourishing dish which can be eaten all year round. Fernande Allard would use a fine Beaujolais to cook the dish and her husband would serve the same wine in the restaurant. Very fresh eggs are easiest to poach, as the white gathers perfectly around the yolk when the egg is slipped into simmering water.

Serves 6

2 bottles (6¼ cups/
1.5 liters) Beaujolais

4 sugar lumps

¼ cup/50 ml brandy

5 ounces/150 g fatty bacon,
about 5 thick strips or
10 thin strips

3 large onions

2 garlic cloves

4 fresh flat leaf parsley sprigs

2 tablespoons/30 g sweet butter

2 tablespoons vegetable oil

3 pounds/1.5 kg boneless
stewing veal, cubed

3 tablespoons all-purpose flour

2 tablespoons tomato paste

1 bouquet garni

½ teaspoon white vinegar

6 very fresh eggs

coarse salt and freshly
ground pepper

Preparation time: 15 minutes
Cooking time: about 1½ hours

Pour the wine into a large pan and add the sugar lumps. Bring to a boil over a low heat, then add the brandy. Bring back to a boil, then set the brandy alight. Let the flames die down, then set aside.

Dice the bacon. Peel and finely chop the onions and garlic. Wash and dry the parsley, then chop.

Heat the butter and oil in a large skillet over medium heat. Add the veal, in batches, and cook, stirring frequently, until browned all over. Remove with a slotted spoon and drain on paper towels. Transfer the veal to a flameproof casserole.

Add the bacon to the skillet and cook until it begins to crisp. Transfer to the casserole. Add the onions to the skillet and cook, stirring occasionally, until translucent, then transfer to the casserole.

Set the casserole over medium heat, sprinkle in the flour, and cook, stirring constantly, for 2–3 minutes. Add the tomato paste, garlic, and bouquet garni. Season with coarse salt and freshly ground pepper. Stir in the wine mixture. Cover and simmer very gently for about 1 hour.

With a slotted spoon, transfer the veal and bacon to a deep serving dish and keep warm. Return the casserole to medium heat and cook until the sauce is reduced and coats the back of a spoon.

Meanwhile, poach the eggs. Fill a sauté pan with water and set over medium heat. When the water begins to simmer, add the vinegar and a little coarse salt. Break the eggs, 1 at a time, into a small bowl or cup. Swirl the water with a spoon and slide the egg into it. Poach for 3 minutes. As each egg is poached, remove with a slotted spoon and let drain on a dishtowel.

Pour the reduced sauce through a fine strainer onto the veal. Place the poached eggs on top, then sprinkle with the chopped parsley, and serve immediately.

Les mères Allard

Potato gratin

This luscious *Gratin de pommes de terre* should be made with a firm, waxy potato variety, such as *Charlotte*, *Belle-de-Fontenay*, *Yukon Gold*, or *Round Red*. Buy good-quality cheese and grate it only at the last minute. Ready-grated cheese is always dry and tasteless. Using freshly grated *Comté* also means that you do not have to dot the top of the gratin with butter for it to turn a beautiful golden color.

Peel and wash the potatoes. Drain them and leave to dry on a dishtowel. Slice the potatoes into thin rounds, rinse, and dry them again.

Pour the milk into a large, heavy pan. Season with salt, freshly ground pepper, and grated nutmeg. Peel the garlic and crush it with a press straight into the milk. Add the potatoes, cover, and cook over low heat, stirring occasionally, for 30 minutes.

Lightly grease a shallow, ovenproof dish with butter. Coarsely grate the cheese.

Pour off most of the milk from the potatoes. Make a layer of potatoes in the prepared dish. Pour one-third of the crème fraîche over them, then sprinkle with one-third of the cheese. Make another 2 layers in the same way, ending with cheese.

Bake in a preheated oven, 475°F/240°C/gas mark 9, for 10–15 minutes, until the top is golden brown and bubbling. Serve.

It is better to brown the gratin in a very hot oven than to place it under a broiler: Broiling makes the top of the gratin dry out.

Serves 6–8

4½ pounds/2 kg waxy potatoes
6¼ cups/1.5 liters milk
freshly grated nutmeg
2 garlic cloves
butter, for greasing
4 ounces/120 g Comté cheese
or Swiss cheese
1¼ cups/300 ml thick
crème fraîche
salt and freshly ground pepper

Preparation time: 15 minutes
Cooking time: about 45 minutes

Les mères Allard

Artichoke omelet

The first globe artichokes of the season are small with tender hearts. Their tapering leaves have needle-sharp points. Mère Barale would also make Omelette aux artichauts using little green Provencal artichokes, which have no choke. This omelet is delicious served cold with mixed baby salad greens.

Serves 3

1 large onion

2 garlic cloves

⅔ cup/150 ml olive oil

10 baby globe artichokes

6 eggs

salt and freshly ground pepper

mixed salad greens, to serve

Preparation time: 10 minutes

Cooking time: about 35 minutes

Peel and finely chop the onion. Halve the garlic cloves. Heat half the olive oil in a skillet over high heat. Add the onions and garlic, lower the heat, and cook, stirring occasionally, for 10 minutes.

Remove the stems and the outer leaves from the artichokes. Trim off the sharp points of the leaves with a sharp knife or kitchen scissors. Slice the artichokes into thin sections and add them to the skillet. Mix the artichokes with the onions and cook over low heat, stirring frequently, for 20 minutes. Season to taste with salt and freshly ground pepper.

Remove the skillet from the heat. Lift out and discard the garlic halves. Break the eggs into a bowl and season with salt and pepper. Add the artichoke mixture to the eggs and beat vigorously.

Pour the remaining oil into the skillet and set over very high heat. Pour in the egg mixture. Using a wooden spoon, push the egg mixture from the outer edge of the skillet into the center. Do this several times until the underside of the omelet is set, but the center is still runny and moist. Fold the omelet over and slide it onto a serving dish. Serve hot or cold with mixed salad greens.

La mère Barale

Swiss chard omelet

The Niçois love Swiss chard ("blea") and often buy slices of this omelet ready-made from street vendors in the old quarter of Nice. This delicious Omelette aux blettes is eaten cold, making it an ideal picnic food. Depending on the recipe, the chard leaves are added to the eggs either raw or cooked. Mère Barale preferred to cook her chard first.

Serves 3

2¼ pounds/1 kg Swiss chard

2 large onions

2 garlic cloves

⅔ cup/150 ml olive oil

3 bay leaves

6 eggs

generous ¾ cup/80 g freshly grated Fribourg cheese or Swiss cheese

salt and freshly ground pepper

mixed salad greens, to serve

Preparation time: 20 minutes

Cooking time: about 40 minutes

Cut off the stems of the chard (you can use them in another recipe). Blanch the leaves in boiling water for 1 minute. Drain, refresh in cold water, then drain again. Chop finely.

Peel and finely chop the onions. Peel and halve the garlic cloves. Pour half of the olive oil into a skillet and set over very high heat. Add the onions and garlic, lower the heat, and cook gently, stirring occasionally, for about 10 minutes.

Add the bay leaves and the chopped chard leaves. Season to taste with salt and pepper. Stir well and cook over a low heat for 20 minutes more.

Break the eggs into a bowl. Remove the skillet from the heat. Remove and discard the bay leaves and garlic pieces. Add the chard mixture and grated cheese to the eggs and beat thoroughly with a fork.

Pour the remaining olive oil into the skillet and set over high heat. Pour in the egg mixture. Using a wooden spoon, push the egg mixture from the edges of the skillet toward the center. As soon as the underside has set and the omelet begins to color, invert a plate over the skillet, and flip it out. Slide the omelet back in, runny side down. Cook for a few minutes more. When the second side is set and golden, slide it onto a serving dish.

Serve this omelet cold with crisp mixed salad greens.

La mère Barale

Braised beef Niçoise style

A strong flavor of ceps characterizes this Daube à la niçoise. Hélène Barale would always make it in large quantities, as she would use any leftovers, mixed with dark green chard, as a filling for her delicious ravioli. The dish cannot be hurried—it must be cooked gently for a long time.

The previous evening, put the dried mushrooms in bowl of cold water to soak.

Next day, peel and slice the onions, garlic cloves, and carrots. Cut the bacon into small dice. Heat the oil in a flameproof casserole, add the beef slices and bacon, and cook, stirring occasionally, for about 7 minutes.

Add the carrot, onions, and garlic and cook, stirring occasionally, for 8 minutes more, until the beef is browned on all sides and the onion is softened. Drain the mushrooms and stir them into the casserole.

Meanwhile, cut a small cross in the top of the tomatoes, put them into a bowl, and cover with boiling water for just a few seconds. Drain, peel, quarter, and seed them. Stir the tomato flesh into the casserole and simmer for 30 minutes.

Pour in the red wine and add the bouquet garni. Simmer for 30 minutes more.

Pour in the brandy. If there is not enough liquid just to cover the meat, add a little water. Season with salt and freshly ground black pepper. Gradually, bring to a boil, then reduce the heat, cover, and simmer for about 3 hours.

Remove and discard the bouquet garni and skim off any fat from the surface. Taste and adjust the seasoning. Serve the braised beef straight from the casserole with freshly cooked pasta drizzled with olive oil.

Serves 6

2½ cups/150 g dried cep mushrooms (porcini)
2¼ pounds/500 g onions, about 7 medium
5 garlic cloves
5 ounces/150 g carrots, about 2 large
9 ounces/250 g fatty bacon, about 9 thick strips or 18 thin strips
7 tablespoons olive oil
3 pounds/1.5 kg beef chuck, sliced into 5 ounce/150 g pieces
3 pounds/1.5 kg tomatoes, 9–10 medium
2¼ cups/500 ml red wine
1 bouquet garni (parsley sprigs, bay leaf, thyme, rosemary)
⅔ cup/150 ml brandy
salt and freshly ground black pepper
freshly cooked pasta, to serve

Preparation time: 15 minutes
Soaking : 12 hours
Cooking time: about 4½ hours

La mère Barale

Breaded lamb chops, Niçoise style

A summery dish, Côtelettes d'agneau panées à la niçoise is delicious eaten hot or cold. Mère Barale preferred to use Fribourg cheese instead of Parmesan, as it melts better. The fresh Provencal herbs that flavor the omelet must be chopped as finely as possible.

Serves 6

5 eggs

1–1¼ cups/65–75 g dry bread crumbs

12 lamb rib chops

7 tablespoons olive oil

½ teaspoon chopped fresh mixed herbs (thyme, rosemary, and bay leaves)

½ cup/50 g freshly grated Fribourg cheese or Swiss cheese

salt and freshly ground pepper

rice or mixed salad greens garnished with chervil, to serve

Preparation time: 10 minutes
Cooking time: 7 minutes
Chilling: 30 minutes

Break the eggs into a wide, shallow bowl and beat them with a fork. Spread the bread crumbs on a plate .

Season the lamb chops with salt and pepper. Dip the chops, 1 at a time, into the beaten eggs, then roll them in the bread crumbs to coat. Place on a plate and chill in the refrigerator for at least 30 minutes to set the crumb crust.

Pour the olive oil into a heavy skillet large enough to hold all of the chops in a single layer and set it over very high heat. Add the chops and cook for about 2 minutes on each side, until browned. Lower the heat to medium.

Mix the chopped herbs and grated cheese into the eggs, whisking well with a fork. Season with salt and pepper. Pour the eggs evenly over the chops. Cover the skillet and remove from the heat. Let it rest, covered, for a few minutes; there will be enough residual heat to finish cooking the thin omelet.

Transfer the chops to a serving dish. Serve warm with rice or cold with mixed salad greens garnished with chervil.

La mère Barale

Stuffed lamb chops

This recipe for Côtelettes d'agneau farcies, chops stuffed with a delicate, savory combination of truffles, mushrooms, and ham, comes straight from Elisa Blanc's notebook. The truffles can be omitted if you like.

Rinse the caul fat in cold water. Pat dry and cut into 8 pieces, each the size of a chop.

Make a white sauce. Melt 1 tablespoon/ 15 g of the butter in a heavy pan over low heat. Add the flour, and cook, stirring constantly, for 1–2 minutes. Gradually pour in the milk, whisking constantly until the sauce begins to bubble. Cook for 2 minutes more, still whisk ing constantly. Season with salt, pepper, and grated nutmeg. Remove the pan from the heat.

Wipe the mushrooms and finely chop them. Melt the remaining butter in a skillet and sauté the mushrooms for 3–4 minutes.

Finely chop the truffle. Add to the skillet with the chopped chicken breast meat and ham and stir in 3–4 tablespoons of the white sauce. Adjust the seasoning.

Place a spoonful of the stuffing on top of each chop, dividing it equally among them. Wrap the chops in the pieces of caul fat.

Vigorously whisk the egg white in a wide, shallow bowl. Spread out the bread crumbs on a plate. Dip the chops, 1 at a time, first in the egg white, then in the bread crumbs to coat. Place the chops on a plate and chill in the refrigerator for at least 1 hour to set the crumb coating.

Melt 2 tablespoons/30 g of the butter in a skillet over low heat. Add the stuffed chops and cook for about 15 minutes, turning them over 2–3 times so that they are evenly browned. Transfer the chops to a warmed serving platter and keep warm.

Pour off the fat from the skillet. Return the skillet to high heat, pour in the white wine, and bring to a boil. Add the water, then boil until reduced.

Whisk in the remaining butter until it is fully incorporated and the sauce is thickened and smooth. Spoon the sauce over the lamb chops and serve immediately.

Serves 4

1 large piece lamb or pork caul fat

8 rib lamb chops, trimmed

1 egg white

1 cup/65 g dry bread crumbs

6 tablespoons/80 g sweet butter

7 tablespoons dry white wine

2 tablespoons water

For the stuffing

2¼ tablespoons/35 g sweet butter

generous ¼ cup/30 g all-purpose flour

scant 1 cup/200 ml milk

pinch of freshly grated nutmeg

1⅓ cups/80 g crimini mushrooms

1 small truffle

½ cup/80 g finely chopped cooked chicken breast meat

½ cup/80 g finely chopped unsmoked ham

salt and freshly ground black pepper

Preparation time: 20 minutes

Chilling: 1 hour

Cooking time: about 30 minutes

La mère Blanc

Pike quenelles with financière sauce

Although no individual can be identified as the inventor of Quenelles de brochet financière, this inspired dish first appeared on menus in Lyons around 1820. The ready-made quenelles sold by gourmet food stores can never replicate the velvety texture of fresh quenelles prepared at home.

Serves 4

For the quenelles
6 tablespoons/80 g butter
1 cup/250 ml milk
freshly grated nutmeg
generous 1 cup/125 g all-purpose flour
5 eggs
9 ounces/250 g pike fillet
2–3 tablespoons crème fraîche
salt and freshly ground pepper

For the sauce
2 tablespoons vegetable oil
2¼ pounds/1 kg chicken necks, backs, and wings
1 onion
½ carrot
1 celery stalk
½ leek
1 bouquet garni
¼ cup/50 g softened butter
2 tablespoons tomato paste
1 tablespoon all-purpose flour
5 tomatoes
½ cup/50 g pitted green olives
3⅔ cups/250 g crimini mushrooms
juice of ½ lemon
coarse salt

Preparation time: 35 minutes
Cooking time: about 3 hours

First make the sauce. Heat the oil in a large flameproof casserole, add the chicken pieces, and cook over medium heat, turning frequently, until browned all over. Pour off the cooking fat.

Peel the onion and carrot and cut into large dice. Dice the celery. Add the onion, carrot, celery, leek, bouquet garni, and half the butter to the casserole. Cook for about 4–5 minutes, then stir in the tomato paste. Cook, stirring constantly, for 2 minutes, then add the flour, and cook for 2 minutes.

Pour in enough cold water to cover the chicken pieces. Quarter the tomatoes and add them to the casserole. Bring to a boil, then reduce heat, and simmer very gently for 3 hours.

Strain the stock through a fine strainer and return it to the casserole. Bring to a boil, then cook until it is reduced and thick enough to coat the back of a spoon. Stir in the green olives.

To make the quenelles, put the butter and milk into a heavy pan. Season with salt, pepper, and grated nutmeg. As soon as the milk boils, add the flour all at once and beat vigorously. Lower the heat and stir constantly with a spatula until the paste starts to pull away from side of the pan. Remove the pan from the heat and beat in 3 of the eggs. Mix thoroughly, cool, and then chill the panada in the refrigerator.

Using tweezers, carefully remove any remaining bones from the pike fillet. Pass the fish through the fine disk of a food mill. Season to taste with salt, pepper, and a pinch of grated nutmeg.

Combine 9 ounces/250 g of the chilled panada with the fish purée. Add the remaining eggs and beat to a smooth paste. Mix in 2–3 tablespoons crème fraîche. Chill until required.

Trim and wash the mushrooms. Pat dry, then quarter them. Put the mushrooms into a pan with a little water, the remaining butter, and the lemon juice. Cook for about 10 minutes, then add them to the sauce.

With wet hands, shape the fish mixture into quenelles—small logs. As each one is shaped, place it on baking parchment.

Bring a large pan of water to a boil, add a handful of coarse salt, and lower the heat to a very gentle simmer. Slide 2—3 quenelles at a time into the simmering water and poach for 15–20 minutes, until they rise to the surface. Remove with a slotted spoon and drain on paper towels. When all of the quenelles have been poached, transfer them to a warmed, deep serving dish and spoon the sauce over them. Serve immediately.

La mère Blanc

Crayfish cooked in Pouilly-Fuissé

When Écrevisses à la nage au pouilly-fuissé is prepared a day in advance, it is even more delicious, as the crayfish have the time to absorb more flavor. The crayfish should be gently warmed before being bathed in the aromatic stock. Serve with toasted country bread and fresh sweet butter.

Serves 4
1 lemon
1 onion
3 carrots
2 shallots
2 bottles (6¼ cups/1.5 liters) Pouilly-Fuissé or Chardonnay
2¼ cups/500 ml water
1 bouquet garni
1 clove
25 black peppercorns
⅓ cup/50 g coarse salt
2¼ pounds/1 kg live crayfish

Preparation time: 40 minutes
Cooking time: about 40 minutes

Remove the rind and the pith of the lemon with a sharp knife. Peel and slice the onion, carrots, and shallots.

Pour the wine and water into a large pan. Add the bouquet garni, vegetables, lemon, clove, peppercorns, and coarse salt. Simmer the court-bouillon for 30 minutes, then remove from the heat, and let cool.

Just before cooking them, gut the crayfish by twisting the central plate of the tail and pulling out the black vein.

Bring the court-bouillon to a boil and throw in all the crayfish at once. After the court-bouillon has returned to a boil, cook for a further 2 minutes. Remove from the heat and set aside to cool.

Remove the crayfish from the court-bouillon and place them on a serving dish. Strain the court-bouillon, reserving the vegetables. Sprinkle the vegetables over the crayfish. Warm the court-bouillon and pour it over the crayfish. Serve immediately.

La mère Blanc

Snails in herb butter

A harmonious combination of garlic, shallots, parsley, and ground almonds gives this version of the classic Escargots de Bourgogne au beurre d'herbes its special flavor. Georges Blanc, who used to make vast quantities of the herb butter, recalls smoothing the butter into each snail with a tiny spatula.

Serves 12

12 dozen prepared canned snails

For the herb butter

4½ **cups**/1 kg sweet butter, softened

1¼ pounds/500 g fresh flat leaf parsley

½ unwaxed lemon

3 tablespoons ground almonds

dash of dry white wine

3¾ ounces/100 g shallots

5 garlic cloves

2 tablespoons/25 g salt

1 teaspoon freshly ground black pepper

Preparation time: 45 minutes

Cooking time: about 12 minutes

Cream the butter. Remove the parsley leaves from the stalks. Wash and dry them. Measure out 11 cups/300 g of leaves and chop them finely. Scrub the skin of the lemon half. Finely grate the rind over the butter. Add the ground almonds and a dash of white wine and mix well.

Peel and finely chop the shallots and garlic cloves. Combine with the chopped parsley and beat into the butter mixture. Season with the salt and pepper.

Drain the snails. Insert a little herb butter into each shell. Insert the snail and seal with more herb butter. Smooth the butter over the opening with a spatula. Chill the stuffed snails until you are ready to cook them.

Place the snails in a shallow ovenproof dish. Bake in a preheated oven, 350°F/180°C/gas mark 4, for about 12 minutes, until the butter is bubbling gently. Serve the snails immediately.

La mère Blanc

Frogs' legs sautéed
with herbs

These days, frogs' legs can be bought, ready to cook, from specialty stores. For Cuisses de grenouille sautées aux fines herbes, the legs are dusted with flour and fried in sizzling hot butter so that they develop a delicious crust.

Rinse, drain, and thoroughly dry the frogs' legs. Set aside.

Pick the leaves off the chervil and parsley stems. Wash and dry them, then chop finely. Peel and finely chop the garlic cloves. Combine the herbs and the garlic.

Lay a large piece of baking parchment on the counter. Place the frogs' legs on the parchment and dust them with flour. Turn them over to dust the other sides. Shake off any excess flour.

Place 2 large skillets on high heat and melt a fourth of the butter in each skillet. When the butter has begun to sizzle, add the frogs' legs. Season with salt and pepper.

As soon as the legs have turned a light golden color, turn them over. Lower the heat and add some more butter. The additional butter will help to lower the temperature in the skillet and keep the fat from burning. The butter must not burn; by the time the legs are cooked, it should have attained a nutty color.

Transfer the frogs' legs to a large, very hot, flameproof dish. Pour some of the butter from the skillets over the legs. Place the dish over high heat and add the remaining butter, a little at a time, so that it foams. Sprinkle with the garlic and herb mixture, stir, and serve immediately.

Serves 4

1¾ pounds/800 g frogs' legs

1 bunch of fresh chervil

1 bunch of fresh parsley

4 garlic cloves

2 tablespoons all-purpose flour

1½ cups/350 g butter

salt and freshly ground pepper

Preparation time: 15 minutes
Cooking time: about 10 minutes

La mère Blanc

Gratin of tripe with white wine and aromatic herbs

Tripes gratinées au vin blanc et aux aromates was the specialty of the house at the Blanc family restaurant in Vonnas. Just before serving, Paulette Blanc would pour hot melted butter over the tripe.

Serves 6

2 large onions

2 shallots

3¼ pounds/1.5 kg tripe

scant 1 cup/200 g butter

1 fresh thyme sprig

1 bay leaf

4 cups/1 liter white wine, such as Mâcon Blanc

chicken stock (optional)

pinch of 4-spice mixture (a mixture of ground pepper, grated nutmeg, ground cloves, and ground cinnamon)

4 carrots

1 bunch of fresh chives

1 tablespoon finely chopped fresh chervil

1 tablespoon finely chopped fresh tarragon

4 tablespoons dried bread crumbs

salt and freshly ground pepper

Preparation time: 20 minutes

Cooking time: 3 hours

Peel and finely chop the onions and shallots. Cut the tripe into ¼-inch/5-mm wide strips.

Melt ⅔ cup/150 g of the butter in a flameproof casserole over medium heat. When the butter begins to sizzle, add the onions and shallots and cook until just beginning to color. Add the tripe, thyme, and bay leaf, stirring well to make sure that the tripe is coated with butter. Pour in the white wine, then add water or chicken stock or a mixture to cover. Season with salt, pepper, and 4-spice mixture. Mix well and gradually bring to a boil. Lower the heat, cover, and simmer gently for 3 hours.

Meanwhile, peel and slice the carrots. Add them to the tripe halfway through the cooking time.

Finely chop the chives. When the tripe has finished cooking, sprinkle it with the chervil, tarragon, and chives. Mix well and transfer to a shallow flameproof dish.

Melt the remaining butter over low heat. Sprinkle a layer of bread crumbs over the tripe, drizzle with the melted butter, and place the dish under a preheated broiler or in a very hot oven.

When the topping has browned, serve the tripe immediately.

La mère Blanc

Braised calf's head with baby vegetables

Braisé de tête de veau aux petits légumes works best with prepared calf's head ready-rolled into a roast. Tender, succulent, and flavorful, calf's head was a popular dish in the eighteenth century. It is less common these days, but connoisseurs continue to appreciate its special qualities.

First, make the flavoring mixture. Peel and finely dice the carrots, onions, and shallots. Dice the celery. Separate and peel the garlic cloves, but leave them whole. Quarter the tomatoes.

Melt the butter in a large, flameproof casserole over medium heat. Add the diced vegetables, garlic cloves, bay leaf, thyme, and cloves and sauté, stirring constantly, for 5 minutes.

Heat 2 tablespoons of the butter with the oil in a skillet over medium heat. Gently brown the calf's head on all sides. Place it on top of the flavoring mixture and cook for 5 minutes more. Pour in the Madeira and vermouth, bring to a boil, and set alight. As soon as the flames die down, pour in the white wine and boil until reduced by one-third. Season with salt and pepper. Add the stock, cover, and simmer gently over low heat for about 1½ hours. Turn the meat over several times so that it cooks evenly.

To make the vegetable garnish, peel the carrots and turnips and slice them into neat ovals, each about the size of a quarter turnip. Cook them in boiling salted water for about 15 minutes. Drain.

Peel the pearl onions. Put them in a pan with just enough cold water to cover. Add half the butter and a pinch of sugar. Season with salt and pepper. Cover the onions with a piece of baking parchment and cook over low heat until almost all of the water has evaporated.

Wash the mushrooms, pat dry, and sauté them in the remaining butter.

Transfer the calf's head roast onto a large serving dish. Cover with a piece of foil and keep warm.

In a bowl, make a paste of 1 tablespoon of the remaining butter and the flour. Add a small ladleful of the cooking liquid and combine thoroughly, then pour the mixture into the casserole. Whisk to combine and simmer for a few minutes. Continue whisking as you add the remaining butter in small pieces. Adjust the seasoning.

Cut the string tying the roast and cut the meat into slices. Arrange them on a warmed serving plate. Strain the sauce through a fine stainer onto the slices of meat. Arrange the vegetable garnish around the meat, garnish with sprigs of fresh chervil, and serve immediately.

Serves 4

⅔ cup/150 g sweet butter

¼ cup/50 ml vegetable oil

2¼ pounds/1 kg prepared calf's head, rolled into a roast

4 tablespoons Madeira

4 tablespoons Noilly Prat or other dry white vermouth

1¼ cups/300 ml dry white wine

4 cups/1 liter chicken stock or beef stock

2 tablespoons all-purpose flour

salt and freshly ground pepper

½ bunch of fresh chervil, to garnish

For the flavoring mixture

2 carrots

2 onions

4 shallots

1 celery stalk

1 garlic bulb

2 tomatoes

1½ tablespoons/20 g sweet butter

½ bay leaf

1 fresh thyme sprig

2 cloves

For the vegetable garnish

5 ounces/150 g baby carrots

5 ounces/150 g small turnips

generous 1 cup/100 g pearl onions

¼ cup/50 g sweet butter

pinch of confectioners' sugar

1½ cups/100 g crimini or portobello mushrooms

salt and freshly ground pepper

Preparation time: 30 minutes

Cooking time: about 2¼ hours

La mère Blanc

Bresse chicken in a creamy sauce

Poulet de Bresse à la crème is the recipe that made Mère Blanc and later, Paulette Blanc, famous. The caramelized sediment stuck on the base of the sauté pan gives the sauce its rich flavor. Although no chicken stock is used, the sauce is extremely flavorful.

Serves 4

1 onion

10 crimini mushrooms

2 garlic cloves

scant ½ cup/100 g sweet butter

1 × 4 pound/1.8 kg chicken
(Bresse chicken was used in the
original recipe), cut into pieces

1 bouquet garni

scant 1 cup/200 ml dry
white wine

4 cups/1 liter crème fraîche

juice of ½ lemon

salt and freshly ground pepper

Vonnas crêpes (see page 107) or
buttered rice, to serve

Preparation time: 15 minutes
Cooking time: about 45 minutes

Peel and quarter the onion. Trim the stems and wash the mushrooms. Pat dry, then then quarter them. Crush the garlic cloves with the flat side of a knife.

Melt the butter in a large sauté pan or skillet over high heat. Place the chicken pieces in the pan and season them with salt and pepper. Add the onion, mushrooms, garlic, and bouquet garni and cook the chicken for 6 minutes on each side. Pour in the white wine and stir well, scraping up all of the caramelized sediment on the base of the pan. Add the crème fraîche and simmer gently for 25–30 minutes.

Transfer the chicken pieces to a warmed deep serving platter. Cover with a piece of aluminum foil and keep warm.

Strain the sauce into a pan through a fine strainer. Add a dash of lemon juice, adjust the seasoning, and bring to a boil.

Pour the sauce over the chicken and serve with Vonnas crêpes or buttered rice.

La mère Blanc

Vonnas crêpes

Mère Blanc's Crêpes de Vonnas are almost like very light fritters. Cooked in clarified butter, these crêpes make an excellent accompaniment to meat or poultry dishes. Sprinkled with sugar or crushed praline, they also make an excellent dessert.

First, clarify the butter. Cut the butter into small pieces and put it in the top of a double boiler or a heatproof bowl set over a pan of barely simmering water. Gradually melt the butter without stirring. The milky solids will fall to the bottom and any impurities will rise to the top.

When it has melted, remove the butter from the heat. Carefully skim off the light colored foam floating on the surface. Spoon off the clarified butter, leaving the milky solids behind. Set aside.

Peel the potatoes. Cook them in boiling. lightly salted water for 25 minutes, or until tender. Drain, then pass through a food mill or potato ricer. Beat in the milk to make a smooth purée. Let cool.

Sift the flour, then mix it into the cooled potato purée. Beat in the whole eggs, 1 at a time, making sure each egg is thoroughly incorporated before adding the next. Add the egg whites and mix well.

Stir in the crème fraîche, 1 spoonful at a time, until the batter has the consistency of light cream. Do not over thin the batter.

Melt 4 tablespoons of the clarified butter in a large skillet over high heat. Pour tablespoonfuls of the batter into the hot butter: They should form neat rounds by themselves. Depending on the size of the skillet, cook 4–6 crêpes at a time. They cook very quickly: As soon as one side is golden, turn the crêpe over and cook the other side.

As the crêpes are cooked, transfer to paper towels to drain. Arrange them on a warm serving platter and keep warm until you are ready to serve.

Serves 6

2½ cups/500 g sweet butter

1¼ pounds/500 g mealy potatoes

¼ cup/50 ml milk

3 tablespoons all-purpose flour

3 eggs

4 egg whites

3–4 tablespoons thin crème fraîche

salt

Preparation time: 20 minutes
Cooking time: about 25 minutes

La mère Blanc

Lettuce loaf

Pain de laitue is another recipe from Elisa Blanc's notebook. She would pour a rich meat or poultry reduction over the loaf and serve it as a side dish with roast beef or chicken.

Serves 6

3 lettuces

2 eggs

1½ tablespoons/20 g sweet butter

scant 1 cup/50 g fine dry bread crumbs

For the sauce

6 tablespoons/80 g sweet butter

scant ⅔ cup/70 g all-purpose flour

4 cups/1 liter milk

freshly grated nutmeg

salt and pepper

Preparation time: 20 minutes

Cooking time: about 1½ hours

First, make the sauce. Reserve 1 tablespoon/ 15 g of the butter and melt the remainder in a pan over low heat. When the butter begins to spit, add the flour all at once, and cook for 2–3 minutes, stirring vigorously. Add the milk and whisk rapidly to prevent lumps from forming. Simmer, stirring constantly, for a few minutes. Season with salt, pepper, and grated nutmeg. Remove the pan from the heat and melt the reserved butter over the surface to prevent a skin from forming.

Separate the lettuce leaves. Set the hearts aside to use in a salad. Using a small knife, trim the edges of the lettuce leaves, then wash, and pat dry. Blanch the leaves for 2 minutes in boiling salted water. Drain. Place the leaves in a food processor and process to a purée.

Stir the lettuce purée into the sauce. Beat in the eggs, making sure that they are fully incorporated. Adjust the seasoning.

Generously grease a charlotte mold or soufflé dish with the butter and coat the base and side with a thin layer of bread crumbs. Tip out any excess.

Pour the lettuce purée into the prepared dish. Put the dish in a bain marie or roasting pan, adding hot water to come halfway up the sides of the dish. Bake in a preheated oven, 300°F/150°C/gas mark 2, for about 1 hour. Check the water level occasionally and add more if necessary.

Unmold the lettuce loaf onto a serving dish. Let cool slightly, so that it will hold its shape when cut in slices. Serve with roast meat or poultry.

La mère Blanc

Chicken liver patties

Gâteaux de foies blonds was almost as famous as Bresse chicken in a creamy sauce and was always served on Sundays at Vonnas. Elisa Blanc would mix a large spoonful of meat or chicken "jus" into the mixture to enrich its flavor. The unmolded patties would be garnished with cockerels' kidneys and combs—from Bresse roosters, naturally.

First, make the sauce. Cut a cross in the bottom of each tomato. Drop the tomatoes into boiling water for a few seconds, then remove, and immediately refresh them with cold water. Peel and quarter the tomatoes, then seed them. Cut the tomato flesh into large dice.

Heat the half the butter and the oil in a large sauté pan over low heat. Peel and finely chop the shallots. Peel the garlic, but leave the cloves whole. When the butter has melted, add the shallots to the pan and cook until they are just translucent. Stir in the tomato paste and add the diced tomatoes, garlic, bouquet garni, and sugar. Mix well and season with salt and pepper. Bring the sauce to a boil, stirring constantly. Cover, lower the heat, and simmer gently for 30 minutes.

Remove and discard the bouquet garni and garlic. Process the sauce to a purée in a food processor. Cover and keep warm in a bain marie.

Pass the chicken liver's through the fine disk of a food mill. Soak the bread crumbs in ½ cup/120 ml of the milk, then mix them into the puréed chicken livers. Add the eggs and egg yolks, followed by the crème fraîche and the remaining milk. Peel and crush the garlic. Peel and finely chop the shallot. Add the garlic and shallot, with the chopped parsley, to the liver mixture. Season with salt, pepper, and grated nutmeg. Mix well. Test the consistency of the mixture by dropping ½ teaspoon of it into a pan of boiling water: It should cook in a round ball without spreading out.

Grease 8 ramekins with butter and divide the liver mixture among them. Place them in a bain marie or roasting pan half-filled with hot water. Bake in a preheated oven, 250°F/120°C/gas mark ½, for 20–30 minutes, or until the point of a sharp knife inserted into a patty comes out dry.

Rinse the mushrooms, pat dry, then quarter them. Melt the remaining butter in a pan and cook the mushrooms for 5 minutes. Add the olives, then stir into the sauce.

Unmold each patty onto a plate and surround with the sauce. Serve immediately.

Serves 8

11 ounces/300 g chicken livers (the original recipe uses livers from Bresse chickens)
2 cups/120 g fresh bread crumbs
3 cups/700 ml milk
3 eggs
3 egg yolks
⅔ cup/150 ml **crème fraîche**
1 garlic clove
1 shallot
2 tablespoons chopped fresh flat leaf parsley
freshly grated nutmeg
butter, for greasing
salt and freshly ground pepper

For the sauce
1¼ pound/500 g tomatoes
3 tablespoons/40 g sweet butter
2 tablespoons olive oil
2 shallots
2 garlic cloves
1 teaspoon tomato paste
1 bouquet garni
1 sugar lump
2¾ cups/200 g crimini mushrooms
12 green olives, pitted and halved
salt and freshly ground pepper

Preparation time: 30 minutes
Cooking time: about 1 hour

La mère Blanc

Chicken in white wine sauce

The Bresse rooster, like all Bresse chickens, has blue legs, white feathers, and a red comb. A plump bird, its flesh is soft and juicy—perfect for Coq au vin blanc. It should be cooked slowly to conserve its delicate texture.

Serves 6

1 × 5½ pound/2.5 kg chicken, cut into pieces

scant 1 cup/200 ml vegetable oil

⅔ cup/150 g butter

9 ounces/250 g chicken necks, backs, wings, and bones

2 tablespoons all-purpose flour

8 tomatoes

½ bunch of fresh parsley

½ bunch of fresh chervil

½ bunch of fresh tarragon

3 shallots

3⅔ cups/250 g crimini mushrooms

1½ cups/350 ml dry white wine

2 tablespoons brandy

salt and freshly ground pepper

Preparation time: 35 minutes

Cooking time: 2 hours

Ask you butcher to remove all the veins in the chicken legs and to cut the thighs and the breast pieces in half.

Heat 7 tablespoons of the vegetable oil and 2 tablespoons/30 g of the butter in a large, flameproof casserole. Add the chicken necks, backs, wings, and bones and cook, turning frequently, for 10 minutes, until golden. Sprinkle in the flour and cook, stirring, until it begins to change color. Pour in just enough water to cover the chicken pieces. Cover and simmer for 45 minutes.

Strain the stock through a fine strainer into a bowl. Set aside.

Cut a cross in the bottom of each tomato. Drop the tomatoes into boiling water for a few seconds. Remove and immediately refresh with cold water. Peel and quarter the tomatoes, then seed them. Dice the tomato flesh.

Wash and dry the parsley, chervil, and tarragon. Pull the leaves off the stems and chop finely. Peel and chop the shallots.

Season the thigh and breast pieces of the chicken with salt and pepper to taste. Heat the remaining oil and 2 tablespoons/30 g of the butter in a flameproof casserole. Cook the thighs for 20 minutes, turning them over to make sure that they are evenly browned. Add the breast pieces and brown them. Lower the heat and cook for 25 minutes more.

Trim the mushrooms and wash under running cold water. Pat dry, then chop them. Add the mushrooms to the casserole with the shallots. Stir to mix, then stir in 1¼ cups/300 ml of of the white wine and the brandy. Boil until the liquid is reduced by half, then add the stock. Bring to a boil. Reduce the heat and simmer for 1 hour.

Remove the pieces of chicken and arrange them on a warmed serving dish. Whisk the remaining butter and remaining wine into the sauce. Stir in the chopped herbs. Pour the hot sauce over the chicken and serve immediately.

La mère Blanc

Mère Blanc's mallard duck

The lakes region near Dombes is full of game. Paul Blanc and his brother would go there to hunt mallard and woodcock. Mère Blanc would only pluck the game after hanging it for a good length of time in her cellar. Many hunters would bring their own game to the restaurant and Mère Blanc would cook it for them in little earthenware pots. The hunters would then pay only a "handling" charge. Colvert façon mère Blanc is one of her famous game dishes.

Peel and finely chop the shallots. Melt 3 tablespoons/40 g of the butter in a flameproof casserole over low heat. Add the shallots and bacon and cook until the shallots are translucent.

Season the duck portions with salt and pepper and add them to the casserole. Cook until lightly browned on all sides, then sprinkle in the flour. Cook, stirring constantly, for 2–3 minutes.

Pour in enough white wine to cover and add the bouquet garni. Bring to a boil, then lower the heat. Cover and simmer gently for about 30 minutes.

Meanwhile, trim and wash the crimini mushrooms. Pat dry. Slice the mushrooms and immediately drizzle them with lemon juice. Melt 2 tablespoons/30 g of the remaining butter in a skillet over medium heat. Add the mushrooms and sauté until they are golden. Season to taste.

Cut the crusts off the bread. Melt the remaining butter in a skillet. When it begins to sizzle, carefully fry the bread until both sides are golden brown.

Put the croûtons on a serving platter. Remove the duck portions from the casserole and place one on each croûton. Keep warm.

Return the casserole to the heat and cook until the sauce has reduced. Skim the fat off the surface and remove and discard the bouquet garni. Stir in the crème fraîche. Bring to a boil and add the mushrooms. As soon as the sauce returns to a boil, spoon it over the duck. Serve immediately.

Serves 4

3 shallots
½ cup/120 g sweet butter
5 ounces/150 g fatty bacon (about 5 thick strips or 10 thin strips), diced
1 × 3 pound/1.4 kg mallard duck or other wild duck, cut into 4 pieces
4 tablespoons all-purpose flour
1 bottle (3 cups/750 ml) dry white wine
1 bouquet garni
scant 4½ cups/300 g crimini mushrooms
juice of ½ lemon
4 slices white sandwich bread
2 tablespoons crème fraîche
salt and freshly ground pepper

Preparation time: 15 minutes
Cooking time: about 50 minutes

La mère Blanc

Veal chops with sorrel

Côte de veau à l'oseille marked a "coming of age" for Georges Blanc. It was the first dish his mother Paulette Blanc allowed him to cook by himself, in 1964, in the kitchen at Vonnas. For the recipe to succeed, it is essential to keep a sharp eye on the veal chops as they cook. The bitterness of the sorrel, which is a perfect accent to the veal, is tempered with cream.

Serves 4

8 large sorrel leaves

4 veal rib chops

2 tablespoons/30 g butter

7 tablespoons dry white wine

1¼ cups/300 ml crème fraîche

salt and freshly ground pepper

Preparation time: 5 minutes

Cooking time: about 12 minutes

Wash the sorrel leaves and pat dry. Remove the stems and cut the leaves into fine strips.

Season the veal chops with salt and pepper. Melt the butter in a skillet over medium heat. Add the chops and cook for 1 minute on each side to seal. Lower the heat and cook the chops for 2–3 minutes more on each side. Transfer the chops to a warmed serving dish, cover, and keep warm.

Pour off the fat from the skillet. Pour in the white wine and stir well, scraping up any sediment on the base of the skillet. Simmer until the liquid is reduced by half, then add the crème fraîche. Cook until the sauce is thick enough to coat the back of a wooden spoon. Adjust the seasoning.

Stir in the strips of sorrel. Pour the sauce over the chops and serve immediately.

La mère Blanc

Bresse turkey stuffed with chestnuts

Dinde de Bresse farcie aux marrons was Paulette Blanc's special Christmas dish and she did not stint on the truffles. She wanted her customers to be amazed by the truffle-scented turkey.

Serves 10

1 × 8¾ pound/4 kg turkey, with its liver

3¾ ounces/100 g veal round steak

3¾ ounces/100 g boneless lean pork

scant ½ cup/100 g shortening

4 shallots

scant 1 cup/200 g sweet butter

1¾ pounds/800 g chestnuts, peeled

1–2 truffles (optional)

1 carrot

1 onion

⅔ cup/150 ml water

salt and freshly ground pepper

salad greens, to serve

Preparation time: 30 minutes

Cooking time: about 3 hours

Ask your butcher to remove the veins from the turkey's thighs. Remove any veins or traces of bile from the turkey liver.

Using a sharp knife, finely chop the veal, pork, shortening, and liver and place in a bowl.

Peel and finely chop 2 shallots. Melt 2 tablespoons/30 g of the butter in a small skillet over medium heat and cook the shallots until they are translucent. Stir the shallots into the chopped meat.

Pass the chestnuts through the medium disk of a food mill. Add them to the stuffing and mix well. Season with salt and pepper. If you like, add 1–2 finely chopped truffles and their juice.

Fill the turkey's cavity with this stuffing. Sew the opening closed with kitchen string and truss the bird. Coat the turkey with butter and place it in a roasting pan.

Peel and dice the carrot, onion, and remaining shallots. Arrange the vegetables around the turkey. Roast the turkey in a preheated oven, 350°F/180°C/gas mark 4, for about 3 hours, basting frequently. As soon as the turkey has browned, cover it with aluminum foil so that it does not burn.

Transfer the cooked turkey to a warm serving dish. Place the roasting pan over medium heat and stir in the water, scraping up the caramelized sediment from the base. Simmer the gravy until slightly reduced. Cut the remaining butter into small pieces and whisk it into the simmering gravy. Pour the gravy into a sauceboat.

Serve each guest with a little breast meat, a little thigh meat, and some of the stuffing, and pour on some gravy. Salad greens with a walnut-oil dressing make the perfect accompaniment.

La mère Blanc

Jugged hare

Delicious and rich, Paulette Blanc's Civet de lièvre with bacon and caramelized pearl onions steeped in sauce is a special treat in the hunting season.

Ask your butcher to cut the hare or jack rabbit into pieces—thighs, forelegs, saddle—and to collect the blood. If it has already been bled, ask for some pork blood—it is needed for the sauce.

Peel the pearl onions. Melt scant ½ cup/100 g of the butter in a large, flameproof casserole. Add the pieces of hare or rabbit, the bacon, and pearl onions and cook until the meat is browned on all sides. Season with salt and pepper. Sprinkle in the flour and cook over low heat until lightly colored.

Peel the garlic cloves, but leave them whole. Pour the wine into a pan and bring to a boil. Set it alight. When the flames have died down, pour the wine into the casserole. Add the bouquet garni and the garlic. Gradually bring to a boil, lower the heat, and simmer gently for 1 hour.

Remove the pieces of hare or rabbit from the casserole and put them into a sauté pan.

In a small bowl, combine the crème fraîche, brandy, and hare's or rabbit's blood. Stir in a small ladleful of the cooking liquid and whisk vigorously to combine. Pour the mixture into the casserole and stir well, then strain through a fine-meshed sieve, and pour it over the hare in the sauté pan. Put the sauté pan over very low heat—the sauce must not boil—and add the bacon and onions. Adjust the seasoning.

Remove the crusts from the bread. Cut each slice of bread in half, diagonally. Melt 2 tablespoons/30 g of the remaining butter in a skillet and fry the bread triangles on both sides until golden. Sprinkle a pinch of chopped parsley on each croûton.

Just before serving, dice the remaining butter and whisk it into the sauce. Put the jugged hare into a warm, deep serving dish, garnish with the croûtons, and serve with fresh egg pasta or boiled potatoes.

Serves 6

1 × 5½ pound/2.5 kg hare or jack-rabbit

1 cup/100 g pearl onions

⅔ cup/150 g sweet butter

5 ounces/150 g fatty bacon, about 5 thick strips or 10 thin strips, diced

3 tablespoons all-purpose flour

3 garlic cloves

2 bottles (6¼ cups/1.5 liters) full-bodied red wine

1 bouquet garni

7 tablespoons crème fraîche

⅔ cup/150 ml brandy

6 slices white sandwich bread

1 tablespoon chopped fresh parsley

salt and freshly ground pepper

fresh egg pasta or boiled potatoes, to serve

Preparation time: 40 minutes
Cooking time: 1¼ hours

La mère Blanc

Sea bass braised in Chablis

André Bourgeois was a connoisseur of fine wines and selected the wines served in the restaurant himself. Every fall, he would attend the Burgundy auction at the Hospice de Beaune and purchase the best vintages. Chablis, a fruity and dry white wine, is a perfect match for fish, especially Loup braisé au chablis. Perhaps this has something to do with the fact that half of the Chablis vineyards have soil derived from fossilized oysters.

Serves 6

7 ounces/200 g onions

1 × 4½ pound/2 kg sea bass, gutted but not scaled

½ bottle (1½ cups/330 ml) Chablis

coarse salt and freshly ground black pepper

For the sauce

5 ounces/150 g shallots

3 fresh tarragon sprigs

1¼ cups/300 ml white wine vinegar

1¼ cups/300 ml Chablis

4½ cups/500 g sweet butter

Preparation time: 15 minutes

Cooking time: about 40 minutes

First, make the sauce. Peel and finely chop the shallots. Put them into a heavy pan. Wash and dry the tarragon, then finely chop the leaves. Pour the vinegar and Chablis into the pan. Add the tarragon. Bring to a boil over low heat and boil until reduced and syrupy.

Dice the butter. Increase the heat to medium and whisk in the butter, 1 piece at a time, until fully incorporated. Strain the sauce through a fine meshed strainer and return it to the pan. Set it in a bain marie to keep warm. Stir the sauce occasionally to prevent it from separating.

Peel the onions and slice into thin rings. Make a bed of onion rings in the base of a large, oval ovenproof dish. Place the sea bass on top of the onions and season to taste with salt and pepper.

Pour the Chablis into a pan and bring to a boil. Boil until reduced by one-third. Pour the wine over the fish. Bake in a preheated oven, 475°F/240°C/gas mark 9, for 20 minutes, basting occasionally.

Remove the fish to a warmed serving platter. Scrape up any caramelized sediment from the base of the dish and strain the cooking liquid through a fine-meshed strainer. Whisk the cooking liquid into the sauce in the bain marie. Pour the hot sauce into a sauceboat and serve immediately with the sea bass.

La mère Bourgeois

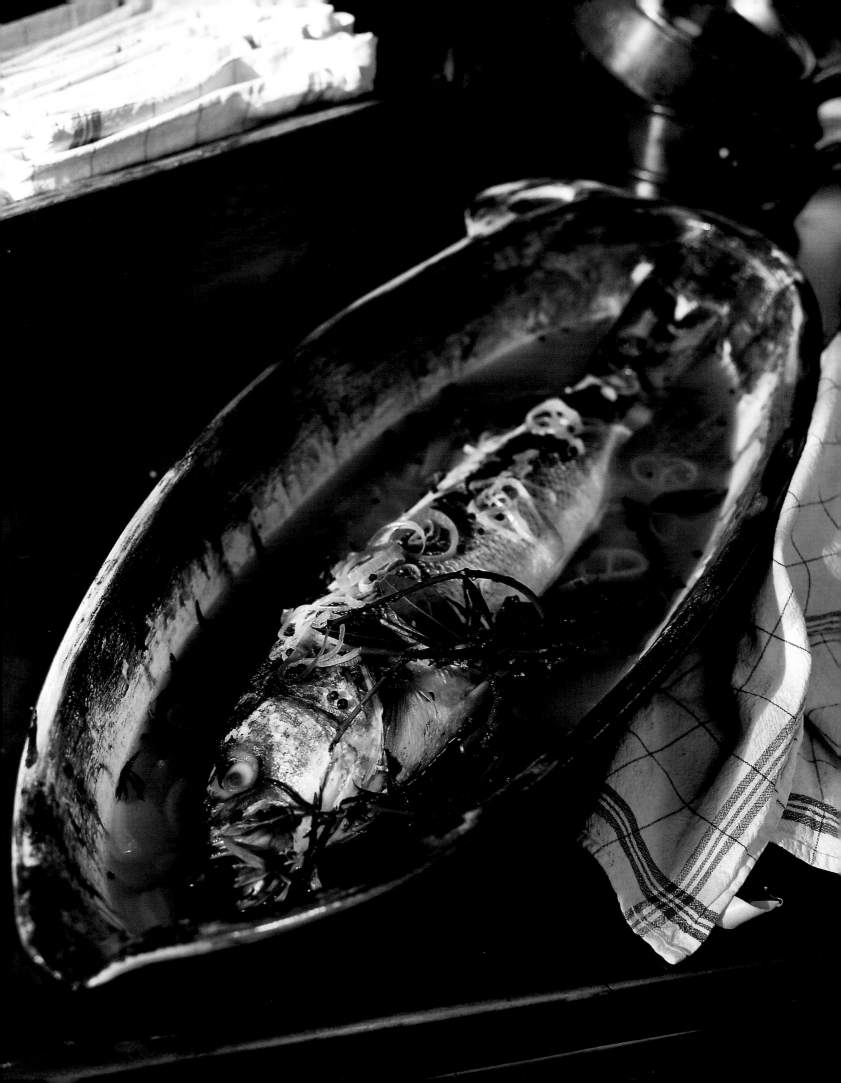

Green beans with foaming butter

Nearly all the inhabitants of Priay were involved in preparing vegetables for the restaurant. Seated on benches in front of their houses, they would slice fresh green beans from the kitchen garden. When serving Haricots verts au beurre mousse, Mère Bourgeois did not stint on the butter. As she used only the finest sweet butter, the finished dish was truly marvelous.

Serves 6
2⅔ cups/400 g green beans
scant ½ cup/100 g sweet butter
coarse salt

Preparation time: 20 minutes
Cooking time: about 8 minutes

Wash and drain the green beans. Trim them, then slice each bean into 4 lengthwise.

Bring a large pan of water to a boil and add some coarse salt. When the water returns to a boil, add the beans and cook for 4–5 minutes, until tender-crisp. Drain the beans and refresh under cold running water. Melt the butter in a skillet over medium heat. As soon as it foams, add the beans and stir to coat them with the butter.

Transfer the beans to a warmed serving dish. Serve them with meat or chicken.

La mère Bourgeois

Baked pike quenelles

Quenelles, like soufflés, should be eaten as soon as they are cooked. Mère Brazier would throw one of her famous tantrums if she spotted that a cooked quenelle had been left standing in the kitchen. She would throw it out immediately and make a fresh one because she insisted that quenelles should be served straight from the oven without delay.

To make the sauce, trim and wash the mushrooms under running cold water, then pat dry. Finely slice and immediately toss with the lemon juice.

Melt 3 tablespoons/40 g of the butter in a large skillet. Add the mushrooms and cook over low heat for about 10 minutes. Season with salt and pepper.

Meanwhile, carefully slide the quenelles into a large pan of lightly salted, barely simmering water. Poach for 5–15 minutes, until they float to the surface. Lift out with a slotted spoon and drain well. Arrange the quenelles in a large, shallow ovenproof dish, leaving plenty of space between them as they will double in size as they cook.

Bring the milk to a boil in a pan. In a bowl, make a paste with the flour and the remaining butter. Stir a spoonful of the hot milk into the paste, then pour the contents of the bowl into the pan, and whisk vigorously until completely smooth.

Stir the crème fraîche into the sauce and season with salt and pepper. Finally, transfer the mushrooms to the sauce, draining them well with a slotted spoon. Bring the sauce to a gentle simmer and pour it over the quenelles.

Bake in a preheated oven, 400°F/200°C/ gas mark 6, for about 25 minutes until golden and bubbling. Serve the quenelles immediately straight from the dish.

Serves 6

6 pike quenelles weighing
3¾ ounces/100 g each

For the sauce

8 cups/500 g crimini mushrooms

juice of ½ lemon

generous ¼ cup/60 g
sweet butter

4 cups/1 liter milk

3 tablespoons all-purpose flour

1 cup/250 ml crème fraîche

salt and freshly ground pepper

Preparation time: 20 minutes

Cooking time: about 40 minutes

La mère Brazier

Black and white chicken

Mère Brazier learned Volaille demi-deuil (literally, "chicken in half-mourning") from the legendary Mère Filloux and it became one of the many dishes that contributed to her fame. Mère Filloux would insist on trussing each chicken herself, so it was a great honor for Eugènie when she was finally entrusted with the operation. The key to the success of the dish lies with the full-flavored, aromatic, poaching stock.

Cut the truffle into ⅛-inch/3-mm thick slices. Gently loosen the chicken's skin by sliding your hand between the skin and the flesh of the breast and thighs. Insert the truffle slices under the skin to make a flat line of truffles along each breast and over each thigh. Be very careful not to tear the skin. Truss the chicken.

Wrap the chicken in a large piece of cheesecloth or a thin dishtowel. Smooth it over the chicken and secure the loose ends of fabric under the wings and thighs with kitchen string.

Peel the carrots and cut them in half. Wash the leeks and cut off the green parts. Tie the whites in a bundle.

Pour the chicken stock into a large Dutch oven or flameproof casserole. Add the chicken—the stock should just cover it. Cover, bring to a boil, then lower the heat, and simmer gently for about 45 minutes. Remove the Dutch oven or casserole from the heat and set aside, still covered, for 30 minutes.

Lift out the chicken and remove the cheesecloth or dishtowel and string. Place the chicken on a serving platter. Undo the bundle of leeks and arrange them with the carrots around the chicken.

Serve immediately with mustard, cornichons, pickled sour cherries, and a small dish of coarse sea salt.

Serves 4–6

1 large truffle
1 × 4 pound/1.8 kg chicken
3 carrots
6 leeks
8 cups/2 liters chicken stock

To serve
mustard
cornichons
pickled sour cherries
coarse sea salt

Preparation time: 20 minutes
Cooking time: about 55 minutes

La mère Brazier

Rhône River Soup

The varied flavors of several types of freshwater fish and shellfish, combined with the gentle bitterness of sorrel in this Soupe du Rhône provide a fine example of the delicacy of Paulette Castaing's cuisine.

Serves 4
2 perch
2 trout
1 small onion
1 leek, white part only
2 garlic cloves
scant 1 cup/100 g sweet butter
8 crayfish
1 cup/250 ml white wine
8 frogs' legs
8 thin slices bread
4 sorrel leaves
2 egg yolks
1 cup/250 ml crème fraîche
salt and freshly ground
black pepper

For the fish stock (makes
4 cups/1 liter)
1½ tablespoons/20 g
sweet butter
2¼ pounds/1 kg fish bones
and trimmings
stems of 1⅓ cups/100 g
mushrooms
1 leek white part only
1 bouquet garni
⅔ cup/150 ml dry white wine
6¼ cups/1.5 liters water
5 black peppercorns
coarse sea salt

Preparation time: 30 minutes
Cooking time: about 1 hour

Ask your fishmonger to fillet the perch and the trout and to give you the bones and fish trimmings.

To make the fish stock, melt the butter in a sauté pan. Add the fish bones and trimmings and stir to mix. Finely chop the mushroom stems. Slice the leek in rounds. Add the mushroom stems and leek to the sauté pan with the bouquet garni and cook, stirring constantly, for 3–4 minutes. Pour in the white wine and water and bring to a boil. Skim the scum from the surface. Season with coarse sea salt and add the black peppercorns. Lower the heat and simmer for 20 minutes.

Remove the stock from the heat and let cool, then strain it through a strainer lined with cheesecloth. Cover and chill in the refrigerator until required.

Peel and finely chop the onion, leek, and 1 garlic clove. Melt the butter in a pan over low heat. Add the onion, leek, and garlic and cook, stirring frequently, until softened, but not brown.

Add the perch and trout bones and trimmings with the crayfish. Cook, stirring constantly, for 5 minutes. Season well with pepper. Pour in the white wine and the fish stock. Bring to a boil, skim the froth, and cook for 20 minutes until reduced.

Arrange the trout and perch fillets and the frogs' legs in a single layer in a large, heavy sauté pan. Season to taste with salt and pepper.

Strain the reduced fish stock onto the fish fillets through a fine-meshed strainer. Set the pan over low heat and simmer very gently for 10 minutes.

Remove the crayfish from the strainer. Break off the tails and remove the black vein. Add the tails to the sauté pan.

Meanwhile, bake the slices of bread in a preheated oven, 350°F/180°C, gas mark 4, until they are golden brown. Transfer them to a small serving dish.

Wash the sorrel leaves and pat dry. Remove the leaves from the stems, fold them in half, and slice into thin strips. Peel the remaining garlic clove and cut it in half. Crush the garlic with the flat side of a knife blade and combine with the egg yolks and crème fraîche.

Divide the fish fillets, crayfish tails, and frogs' legs among 4 wide soup plates.

Pour the egg yolk mixture into the fish stock, whisking briskly to combine; Do not let the mixture boil.

Pour the hot soup over the fish. Garnish with the sorrel chiffonade. Serve immediately with the toasted bread.

La mère Castaing

Calf's sweetbreads with asparagus

Paulette Castaing liked to make Médaillon de ris de veau aux asperges during the all too brief season for wild asparagus. She would also make a variation of the dish using baby fava beans in a parsley sauce.

Soak the sweetbreads in water acidulated with the vinegar for 1 hour.

Drain, then refresh them in cold water. Put the sweetbreads into a pan and cover with cold water. Bring to a boil and add a handful of salt. Poach the sweetbreads for 4 minutes. Drain and refresh with cold water. Drain again and carefully peel off the white membranes. Wrap the sweetbreads in a clean dishtowel and press them under a weighted board.

Trim the stems, then peel the asparagus. Cut off the asparagus tips and cut the stems into small pieces. Melt 1½ tablespoons/20 g of the butter in a flameproof casserole over low heat, add all the asparagus with the sugar, and cook, stirring frequently, for about 5 minutes. Pour in the chicken stock and cook for 30 minutes.

Using a slotted spoon, remove the asparagus tips and set aside. Process the remaining asparagus and stock in a food processor or blender. Rub the purée through a fine-meshed strainer to remove any fibers. Pour it back into the pan and cook over low heat until reduced by half. Adjust the seasoning.

Dissolve the cornstarch in a little cold water. Pour the crème fraîche into a pan and heat gently, then stir in the cornstarch paste. Pour this mixture into the asparagus coulis and mix well.

Cut the sweetbreads into medallions. Melt the remaining butter in a skillet over low heat. Add the medallions and cook for 4–5 minutes on each side, depending on their thickness. Season with salt and freshly ground pepper and arrange the medallions on a serving platter. Arrange the asparagus tips between the medallions.

In a small bowl, whisk the egg yolk with a small ladleful of the asparagus coulis. Pour the mixture back into the coulis, and whisk in a little lemon juice. Spoon the hot sauce over the sweetbreads. Garnish with sprigs of chervil and serve immediately.

Serves 4

1¼ pounds/500 g calf's sweetbreads

1 tablespoon vinegar

3¾ pounds/1.5 kg green asparagus

6 tablespoons/80 g sweet butter

2 sugar lumps

4 cups/1 liter chicken stock

¼ teaspoon cornstarch

scant 1 cup/200 ml crème fraîche

1 egg yolk

juice of ½ lemon

salt and freshly ground pepper

fresh chervil sprigs, to garnish

Preparation time: 20 minutes
Soaking: 1 hour
Cooking time: about 20 minutes

La mère Castaing

Pike-perch "Côtes du Rhône"

Paulette Castaing was captivated by the majestic Rhône River winding its way past the terrace of her inn, the Beau-Rivage. Sandre côtes du Rhône is another recipe inspired by the river—a firm and flavorful pike-perch.

Serves 4

1 × 2½ pound/1.2 kg pike-perch
(if unavailable, use pike or perch)

1 carrot

1 onion

1 garlic clove

1 celery stalk

6 tablespoons/80 g sweet butter

1 bouquet garni

1 bottle (3 cups/750 ml) Côtes-
du-Rhône wine

1 cup/250 ml crème fraîche

4 leeks, white parts only

½ cup/120 ml water

1 shallot

7 ounces/200 g chanterelle
mushrooms

2 fresh flat leaf parsley sprigs

salt and freshly ground
black pepper

10 fresh chervil sprigs, to garnish

Preparation time: 20 minutes
Cooking time: about 45 minutes

Ask your fishmonger to fillet the pike-perch. Also take home the bones, trimmings, and the fish head.

Peel and finely dice the carrot, onion, and garlic. Finely dice the celery. Melt 1 tablespoon/15 g of the butter in a pan over low heat. Add the diced vegetables and the bouquet garni and cook gently until translucent, but not browned.

Add the fish trimmings, bones, and head. Pour in three-quarters of the wine and bring to a boil. Lower the heat, remove the scum, and cook gently for 25 minutes. Strain the stock through a fine-meshed strainer and return it to the pan. Bring back to a boil and reduce slightly.

Pour the remaining wine into a heavy pan and boil to reduce until it has almost dried out—it should be syrupy and shiny. Whisk in the stock and the crème fraîche. Season with salt and pepper and cook until the sauce is thick enough to coat the back of a wooden spoon.

Wash the leeks and cut them into fourths lengthwise. Cut the lengths into small dice.

Melt 1 tablespoon/15 g of the remaining butter in a small sauté pan. Add the leeks, stir, then add the water, and season with salt and pepper. Cover the pan and cook for 9 minutes.

Peel and finely chop the shallot. Trim the the chanterelles, then wipe them clean with paper towels. Melt 1½ tablespoons/20 g of the remaining butter in a skillet over medium heat. Add the mushrooms and cook for 5 minutes.

Add the shallots and cook, stirring occasionally, for 5 minutes more. Season with salt and pepper. Chop the parsley and stir it into the mushroom mixture.

Melt the remaining butter in a nonstick skillet. When the pan is hot, cook the pike-perch fillets for 3 minutes on each side. Season to taste.

Arrange the leeks on a serving platter. Place the pike-perch fillets on top of the leeks, and sprinkle them with the chanterelle mixture. Garnish with chervil leaves. Gently reheat the sauce and serve with the fish.

La mère Castaing

Guinea fowl with green peppercorn sauce

Paulette Castaing nicknamed boneless guinea fowl "pintadons," the diminutive form of "pintandeau" because she felt that they no longer resembled grown guinea fowl— hence the recipe title, Pintadons au poivre vert.

Ask your butcher to halve and part-bone the guinea fowl, leaving the drumsticks intact.

The day before serving, bring the milk to a boil in a pan. Remove from the heat and stir in ¼ cup/60 g of the butter. Season with salt, pepper, and grated nutmeg. Stir in the bread crumbs and set aside until they have absorbed the milk.

Return the pan to medium heat and cook, stirring constantly, until the mixture dries out. Remove the pan from the heat and beat in the egg yolks, followed by the whole eggs, 1 at a time, making sure that each egg is fully incorporated before adding the next. Chill the "dough."

Cut the chicken breast meat into pieces and process in a food processor with scant 1 cup/200 g of the remaining butter and the chilled "dough." Push the mixture through a fine-meshed tamis—drum sieve—into a bowl. (An ordinary strainer will work, but it will take more effort.)

Cut the foie gras into small dice. Drain the green peppercorns. Mix the foie gras and half the peppercorns into the stuffing. Cover with plastic wrap and chill overnight.

Next day, season the guinea fowl halves with salt and pepper. Put a heaping tablespoon of stuffing into each half, and roll up the guinea fowl to enclose—try to retain the shape of the bird. Wrap each half in a strip of bacon and secure with kitchen string. Melt ¼ cup/50 g of the remaining butter in a flameproof casserole over low heat. Brown the guinea fowl halves, then cover, and cook for about 35 minutes.

Remove the birds from the casserole. Remove the string and bacon. Transfer the guinea-fowl to a serving platter and keep warm. Pour off the fat from the casserole.

Return the casserole to the heat and add the wine and water or stock. Bring to a boil and cook until reduced. Dice the remaining butter and whisk it into the sauce. Add a few green peppercorns to taste. Spoon some of the sauce over the guinea fowl.

Pour the rest into a sauceboat and serve immediately with the guinea fowl.

Serves 4

1 × 3¼ pound/1.5 kg guinea fowl
1¾ cups/400 ml milk
1½ cups/350 g sweet butter
freshly grated nutmeg
3½ cups/200 g fresh white bread crumbs
4 egg yolks
2 eggs
9 ounces/250 g chicken breast portions
5 ounces/150 g fresh foie gras
1 small jar green peppercorns
2 long strips lean bacon
7 tablespoons white wine
½ cup/120 ml water or veal stock
salt and freshly ground pepper

Preparation time:
20 minutes, the day before
Cooking time: about 40 minutes

La mère Castaing

Wild duck surprise

When Gisèle Crouzier first made Canard sauvage surprise for her husband, he could not believe his own taste buds. The flavor was delicate, delicious, and extremely surprising. He advised her to write the recipe down immediately without changing a thing. Wild ducks often feed on freshwater fish, but it is daring to cook them with a fish stuffing. Gisèle Crouzier chose to use turbot, a very delicate fish, for this tantalizing and subtle recipe.

Serves 4

2¼ pounds/1 kg live mussels

1¾ cups/400 ml dry white wine, such as Sauvignon Blanc

15 shallots

½ onion

3 garlic cloves

2 tablespoons duck or goose fat or butter

½ teaspoon all-purpose flour

2 oven-ready wild ducks, plus their hearts and livers

4 tablespoons milk

1 cup/50 g fresh white bread crumbs

1 egg

7 ounces/200 g turbot or halibut fillet

1 tablespoon Dijon mustard

1 tablespoon crème fraîche

salt and freshly ground pepper

plain or saffron rice, to serve

Preparation time: 30 minutes

Cooking time: about 40 minutes

Scrape off the mussels' beards. Scrub them in plenty of cold water, then drain. Discard any with damaged shells or that do not shut immediately when sharply tapped. Put the mussels in a large pan with the white wine. Season with a little pepper. Cover and bring to a boil over high heat. Cook, shaking the pan occasionally, for 3 minutes. Drain the mussels, reserving the cooking liquid. Shell the mussels and set them aside.

Peel and finely chop the shallots, onion, and garlic. Melt 1 tablespoon of the fat in a pan over medium heat. Add the shallots, onion, and garlic and cook until translucent. Sprinkle in the flour and cook, stirring constantly, for 2 minutes. Stir in the reserved cooking liquid. Lower the heat and simmer gently for about 20 minutes.

Meanwhile, make the stuffing. Using a sharp knife, finely chop the duck hearts and livers.

Combine the milk and bread crumbs in a bowl and set aside to soak. When all the milk has been absorbed, whisk in the egg. Chop the fish fillet. Mix it into the bread

crumbs with the chopped giblets. Add a few mussels. Season with salt and pepper.

Brush the ducks' cavities with some of the mustard. Divide the stuffing among the birds. Sew the cavities closed with a trussing needle.

Melt the remaining fat over high heat in a flameproof casserole or Dutch oven large enough to hold the 2 birds. Brown the ducks on all sides. Cover and cook for about 20 minutes over medium heat.

Strain the mussel stock and vegetable sauce through a fine-meshed strainer into a pan. Set the pan over low heat and add the crème fraîche, remaining mustard, and the rest of the mussels. Taste and adjust the seasoning, if necessary.

Remove the ducks from the casserole. Slice them in half on a cutting board with channels to catch any juices that run off. Add the juices to the mussel sauce. Put the ducks on a warm platter. Serve the sauce in a separate tureen.

Gisèle Crouzier would serve this dish with plain or saffron rice.

La mère Crouzier

Hare "à la royale"

Lièvre à la royale is a sumptuous recipe from Périgord that Gisèle Crouzier would make during the hunting season. Sometimes, she would simply cook only the saddle of the hare "à la royale" and make a stew with the thighs. She preferred to use partially cooked foie gras in the hare's stuffing since "it would release less fat than raw foie gras" during cooking and would create a firmer stuffing that did not crumble when the hare was carved.

Bone the hare or rabbit, taking care not to pierce the flesh. Remove and finely chop the liver, heart, kidneys, and thigh meat. Put the chopped mixture into a bowl. Add the egg and mix well. Season with salt and freshly ground pepper.

To make the stock, chop the hare or rabbit bones and put them in a stockpot or flameproof casserole. Pour in the white wine and water. Peel and slice the carrot and onion. Add them to the stockpot with the bouquet garni. Bring to a boil over low heat, carefully skimming off all the scum that rises to the surface. Add the peppercorns and a pinch of coarse sea salt. Cover and simmer gently for about 40 minutes.

Lay the boned hare or rabbit flat on a large chopping board. Cut the foie gras into thin sticks. Set a little of the foie gras aside to use in the final thickening of the sauce. Slice the truffles, then cut the slices into strips. Arrange half of the chopped stuffing along the middle of the hare, leaving a border all around. Top with alternating sticks of foie gras and truffle strips. Cover with the remaining stuffing. Gently press the stuffing down with the back of a fork. Using a trussing needle, sew the hare or

rabbit closed, lengthwise. Tie the resulting package like a roast with trussing string.

Melt the duck fat or butter in a flameproof casserole. Add the hare or rabbit and brown all over.

Meanwhile, peel and finely chop the shallots, carrots, and onion. Add them to the casserole. Stir to coat them with the fat, then add the wine, thyme, bay leaf, and parsley. Strain the stock through a fine-meshed strainer into the casserole. Bring to a boil, then reduce the heat. Cover and simmer gently for about 1½ hours, depending on the age of the hare or rabbit.

Remove the hare or rabbit from the casserole, discard all the string, and keep it warm on a platter. Bring the cooking liquid to a boil over high heat until slightly reduced. With a skimmer, remove the herbs. Process the vegetables and the cooking liquid in a blender or food processor, then return to the pan. Mash the reserved foie gras with the back of a fork and whisk it into the sauce. Heat the sauce. Pour a little of it over the hare or rabbit and serve the rest in a sauceboat.

Gisèle Crouzier would serve this dish with chanterelles or truffled potatoes

Serves 6

1 × 3¼ pound/1.5 kg hare or jack-rabbit

1 egg

½ lobe partially cooked foie gras

4 medium-size truffles

2 tablespoons/30 g duck fat or butter

4 shallots

2 carrots

½ onion

2¼ cups/500 ml dry white wine, such as Sauvignon Blanc

1 fresh thyme sprig

1 bay leaf

2 fresh parsley sprigs

salt and freshly ground pepper

For the stock

1 cup/250 ml dry white wine

⅔ cup/150 ml water

1 carrot

1 onion

1 bouquet garni

5 black peppercorns

coarse salt

Preparation time: 50 minutes

Cooking time: about 3 hours

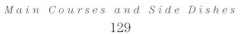

La mère Crouzier

Partridge pie with black salsify

Gisèle Crouzier always preferred the delicate texture and subtle flavor of black salsify to that of regular salsify. Taking her inspiration from the traditional Périgord salsify tart, she developed this recipe—Toutière de perdreaux aux scorsonères. She would make the partridge heads stick out of the pastry and create pastry collars around the necks for a spectacular presentation.

Serves 4

2¼ pounds/1 kg black salsify

juice of 1 lemon

4 cups/1 liter chicken stock

2 tablespoons goose
or duck fat or butter

1 tablespoon all-purpose flour

4 partridges, plucked, dressed,
and trussed

4 purple figs

7 ounces/200 g partially cooked
foie gras

4 confit duck thighs

1 egg

1¼ pounds/500 g puff pastry

salt and freshly ground
black pepper

Preparation time: 30 minutes

Cooking time: about 1 hour

Chilling: 30 minutes

Scrub the salsify in cold water to remove as much dirt as possible. (It is a good idea to wear gloves when dealing with salsify as the milky liquid that oozes when it is peeled is sticky and stains.) With a small knife, peel the black salsify roots and cut them into 2-inch/5-cm sections. As you peel them, put them in a bowl of water acidulated with lemon juice.

Bring the stock and 1 tablespoon of the goose or duck fat or butter to a boil in a large pan. Sift the flour over the surface. Drain the salsify, add to the stock, and cook for about 30 minutes.

Meanwhile, melt the remaining goose or duck fat or butter in a flameproof casserole over high heat. Season the partridges with salt and pepper and brown them in the fat. When they are browned on all sides, cover the casserole and reduce the heat. Cook for about 15 minutes or until the juices run clear when the thickest part is pierced with a fork or the point of a knife.

Remove the partridges from the casserole and pour off the cooking fat. Pour about ⅔ cup/150 ml of the salsify cooking liquid into the casserole and place over high heat. Stir well, scraping up any sediment on the base of the casserole, bring to a boil, and cook until the sauce is reduced to about 8 tablespoons.

Drain the salsify. Divide the pieces among 4 individual ovenproof porcelain pie plates. Wash the figs, pat dry, and cut each one into fourths without cutting all the way through. Squeeze each fig to open it into a star shape. Cut the foie gras into 4 slices.

For each pie, place the fig in the middle of the salsify and season with pepper. Place a slice of foie gras, then a partridge on top. Place a confit duck thigh next to the fig and drizzle with the sauce.

Separate the egg. Brush the outsides and tops of the pie plates with the egg white. Beat the yolk with a few drops of water.

Roll out the puff pastry on a lightly floured surface. Cut 4 rounds of pastry, each at least ¾ inch/2 cm larger in diameter than the pie plates. Place the pastry over the filling and press to seal the edges. Brush the pastry lids with the egg yolk. Chill the pies in the refrigerator for 30 minutes.

Bake the pies in a preheated oven, 425°F/220°C/gas mark 7, for about 20 minutes. Serve the pies hot straight from the oven.

La mère Crouzier

Pike terrine with nasturtiums

One day in April 1977, Gisèle Crouzier's husband brought an enormous 15-pound/ 7.5-kg pike to her kitchen. Gisèle had to come up with a way to cook this huge fish. Inspired by the nasturtiums in flower on that day, she devised this delicate recipe—Terrine de brochet capucine.

Serves 8–10

1 × 5½ pound/2.5 kg pike

4 cups/1 liter fish stock (see page 122)

2 eggs

1 fennel bulb

½ celery root

juice of ½ lemon

10 shallots

4 tablespoons capers

about 12 nasturtium flowers

1 bunch of watercress

salt and freshly ground pepper

For the sauce

2 tablespoons water

2 egg yolks

scant ½ cup/100 g sweet butter

6 tablespoons crème fraîche

¼ cup/50 ml Champagne

2 tablespoons capers

nasturtium flowers

salt and freshly ground pepper

Preparation time: the day before, about 40 minutes

Cooking time: about 1½ hours

The day before, ask your fishmonger to fillet and skin the pike. Ask for the trimmings. Using tweezers, carefully remove any remaining bones from the fillets. Make a stock with the pike trimmings and reduce it to 1 cup/250 ml. Hard-cook the eggs for 12 minutes. Shell and finely chop them.

Wash and dry the fennel bulb and remove the tough outer layers. Peel the celery root. Thinly slice the fennel and celery root, then finely chop. Drizzle the chopped vegetables with lemon juice. Chop 1 of the pike fillets. Peel and finely chop the shallots.

In a large bowl, combine the chopped pike, fennel, celery root, and hard-cooked eggs with the capers and some nasturtium petals. Moisten with a little of the fish stock and mix well. Season with salt and freshly ground pepper.

Cut the other pike fillets into thin slices. In a terrine or loaf pan, make a layer of the chopped mixture. Top this with a layer of pike slices. Continue to alternate the layers, finishing with a layer of the chopped mixture. Pour the remainder of the fish stock over the terrine and bake it in a preheated oven, 325°F/160°C/gas mark 3, for 1 hour. Let the terrine cool to room temperature before covering it with plastic wrap and chilling overnight.

Next day, make the sauce. Pour the water into a heatproof bowl and add the egg yolks. Place the bowl over a pan of barely simmering water and whisk until the mixture begins to thicken. Cut the butter into small pieces and whisk into the sauce, a few pieces at a time. Then whisk in the crème fraîche. Add the Champagne and whisk again. Season to taste.

Chop the capers and remove the petals from a few nasturtium flowers. Add these to the sauce at the last minute.

Wash and dry the watercress. Arrange it around the edge of a platter and sprinkle with nasturtium flowers. Cut the terrine in slices. Arrange these in the center of the platter. Serve the warm sauce separately.

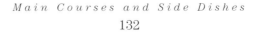

La mère Crouzier

Snail and mushroom pots

Gisèle Crouzier has given us this delicate recipe of Cassolette d'escargots, full of the flavors of fall. Leaving the snails to steep for a long time in the delicious wild mushroom mixture makes sure that they are redolent of the mossy, woody aromas of the forest.

Serves 6

10 shallots

10 garlic cloves

½ bunch fresh flat leaf parsley

1¼ pounds/500 g chanterelles

1¼ pounds/500 g ceps

2¼ pounds/1 kg brown crimini mushrooms

7 tablespoons water

scant ½ cup/100 g butter

scant 1 cup/100 g ground almonds

6 dozen canned snails

salt and freshly ground pepper

Preparation time: 30 minutes

Steeping: 1 hour

Cooking time: about 20 minutes

Peel and finely chop the shallots. Cut each garlic clove in half and remove the shoot. Crush all the garlic with the flat blade of a large knife. Pick the parsley leaves off the stalks. Wash and dry the leaves before finely chopping them.

Wipe the chanterelles and ceps with damp paper towels. Trim the stems. Briefly wash the crimini mushrooms under cold running water and pat dry. Chop all the mushrooms into small pieces.

Pour the water into a casserole. Add the mushrooms, butter, chopped shallots, garlic, ground almonds, and chopped parsley. Cook for about 20 minutes over low heat. Season with salt and pepper. Add the drained snails to the mushroom mixture. Cover and let steep for at least 1 hour.

Just before serving, reheat the snails over very low heat. Divide the snails and the sauce into warmed individual earthenware serving dishes.

La mère Crouzier

Grand mique with veal kidneys and morels

A specialty of the Périgord region, the "mique" is a dumpling that dates from the Middle Ages. Traditionally, a round loaf of dough was cooked by floating it on top of a "pot au feu," "poule au pot," or even a bacon soup. While cooking, the base of the "mique" soaks up some of the broth. Gisèle Crouzier did not like the texture of the soggy bread, so she adopted a different technique, gently frying thick slices of "mique" in butter and serving Mique royale aux rognons de veau et aux morilles.

Make the *mique* the day before. Dissolve the yeast in the water. Add a little flour and stir with your fingers to create a "sponge." Cover with a dishtowel and leave to rise in a draft-free place. The "sponge" is ready when cracks develop on the surface.

Stir in the remaining flour. Add the oil, a pinch of salt, the sugar, and the eggs. Mix to a dough, then knead thoroughly until it is smooth and no longer sticks to your fingers. Form the dough into a ball. Dust a piece of cheesecloth with flour and place the dough in it. Cover the ball with another cloth and set aside in a draft-free place for 1 hour, or until the dough has doubled in bulk.

Bring 8 cups/2 liters of water to a boil in the base of a steamer. Place the dough ball, still wrapped in cheesecloth, in the top of the steamer, cover, and cook for about 30 minutes, or until a toothpick inserted into the *mique* comes out clean. Lift it out of the steamer and remove the cheesecloth. Place it on a wire rack.

Next day, wash the morels and soak them in warm water to cover for 1 hour. Transfer them to another bowl of warm water with a slotted spoon. Strain the water from the first bowl through a cheesecloth-lined strainer and reserve. (Morels must be washed in several changes of water as they are often full of grit.)

Peel and finely chop the shallots. Melt half the butter in a sauté pan and gently cook the shallots over low heat until they are golden. Add 1¼ cups/300 ml of the reserved soaking liquid and bring to a boil. Drain the morels. Stir the crème fraîche and morels into the pan and season with salt and pepper. Simmer gently over low heat for about 30 minutes.

Cut the kidneys into large dice. Melt the remaining butter in a skillet over high heat. Sauté them for 3 minutes, stirring frequently. Season with salt and pepper and combine them with the morels.

Cut the *mique* into ½-inch/1-cm thick slices. Melt the butter in a skillet and brown the slices on both sides. As soon as they are browned, transfer them to a warmed serving dish or onto individual plates. Pour the kidney and morel topping over the *mique* slices and serve immediately.

Serves 6

For the mique
½ ounce/15 g fresh yeast
7 tablespoons lukewarm water
5 cups/500 g all-purpose flour, plus extra for dusting
1 tablespoon vegetable oil
pinch of superfine sugar
6 eggs
¼ cup/50 g sweet butter
salt

For the topping
1¾ cups/100 g dried morel mushrooms
10 shallots
¼ cup/50 g sweet butter
4 cups/1 liter crème fraîche
3 trimmed veal kidneys
salt and freshly ground pepper

Preparation:
the day before, 30 minutes;
on the day, 20 minutes
Rising: 1 hour
Soaking: 1 hour
Cooking time: about 40 minutes

La mère Crouzier

Rabbit Albicocco

"I love apricots because they are sweet and tart at the same time." In June 1969 Gisèle Crouzier devised a recipe combining rabbit and apricots. The director Jean-Gabriel Albicocco was making a movie in the neighborhood at that time and he and his team were staying at "La Croix-Blanche." Coincidentally, Albicocco's name meant "apricot grower" in Italian, so when Gisèle Crouzier asked if she could name the dish, of which he was very fond, Lapin Abicocco, he agreed.

Serves 6

24 dried apricots

2¼ cups/500 ml water

1 tea bag

2 tablespoons apricot preserve

2 carrots

10 shallots

½ onion

2 garlic cloves

1 tablespoon olive oil

1 × 4 pound/1.8 kg rabbit, cut into pieces

1 bouquet garni

2¼ cups/500 ml dry white wine

2¼ cups/500 ml chicken stock

salt and freshly ground pepper

sautéed spinach leaves, to serve

Preparation time: 15 minutes

Soaking: 30 minutes

Cooking time: about 1 hour

Put the dried apricots in a bowl of cold water and scrub them clean. Drain.

Pour the water into a pan, bring to a boil, then add the tea bag. Remove the pan from the heat and let the tea brew for a couple of minutes. Add 1 tablespoon of apricot preserve. Remove and discard the tea bag, add the dried apricots to the pan, and cover. Soak for about 30 minutes.

Return the pan to the heat and cook the apricots over low heat for 10 minutes. Set the pan aside and keep warm.

Peel and finely chop the carrots, shallots, onion, and garlic cloves.

Heat the olive oil in a sauté pan, add the rabbit pieces and cook over medium heat until browned on all sides. Remove the rabbit to a plate. Add the chopped vegetables and garlic to the sauté pan and cook. Return the rabbit pieces to the sauté pan and add the bouquet garni, the remaining apricot preserve, and the soaked apricots. Season with salt and pepper. Add the white wine and chicken stock. Bring to a boil. Reduce the heat and simmer gently for about 45 minutes.

Transfer the rabbit pieces and the apricots to a warmed serving dish. Remove and discard the bouquet garni from the pan. Bring the sauce to a boil and cook until reduced and slightly syrupy. Process the sauce to a purée in a blender or food processor, then reheat. Pour the warm sauce over the rabbit pieces and apricots.

Serve the dish immediately with sautéed spinach leaves.

La mère Crouzier

Tablier de sapeur

The "Chez Léa" restaurant still serves this Lyons specialty. On being served with a piece of fried, crumbed tripe, General Castellane, a great soldier and later, the military governor of Lyons during the reign of Napoleon III, is said to have exclaimed "It looks like my sappers' apron." This unusual name for the dish entered the local vocabulary. Tripe is usually sold already washed and cooked.

Serves 4

1 piece of honeycomb beef tripe

⅔ cup/150 ml white wine, such as Mâcon

1 egg

1 tablespoon Dijon mustard

6 tablespoons dried bread crumbs

1 lemon

¼ cup/50 g clarified butter (see page 107)

salt and freshly ground pepper

For the sauce

1 egg yolk

½ teaspoon Dijon mustard

1 cup/250 ml peanut oil

½ teaspoon red wine vinegar

1 fresh tarragon sprig

5 fresh chervil sprigs

½ bunch of fresh chives

salt and freshly ground pepper

Preparation time: 15 minutes

Marinating: at least 4 hours

Chilling: 1 hour

Cooking time: 10 minutes

Cut the tripe into 4 pieces. Place them on a large platter and drizzle with the white wine. Season with salt and pepper. Place in the refrigerator to marinate for several hours, turning the pieces occasionally.

Whisk the egg with the mustard in a shallow dish. Spread out the bread crumbs on a plate. Drain the tripe and pat the pieces thoroughly dry. One at a time, dip each piece into the egg mixture, then into the bread crumbs. Chill the tripe in the refrigerator for at least 1 hour to prevent the crumbs from falling off during cooking.

Meanwhile, make the sauce. In a bowl, whisk the egg yolk with the mustard. Whisking constantly, add the peanut oil in a thin, steady stream. When the sauce has the consistency of mayonnaise, whisk in the wine vinegar. Pick off the tarragon and chervil leaves. Finely chop them with the chives. Mix the herbs into the mayonnaise. Season to taste with salt and pepper.

Wash and dry the lemon. With a zester, cut lengthwise grooves into the rind. Cut the lemon into thick slices.

Heat the clarified butter in a heavy skillet. When it begins to sizzle, add the tripe and cook for about 5 minutes on each side, until golden brown.

Arrange the tripe on a warmed serving dish. Place a lemon slice on each piece and serve immediately with the sauce.

La mère Léa

"Cervelle de canuts"—
fresh herbed cheese

The "canuts" were silk weavers in Lyons who seemed to survive on a type of fresh cheese called "claqueret". Felix Benoît and Henry Clos-Jouve described it as "a soft, but not too wet, white cheese that one beats like one beats one's wife. When the cheese is thoroughly beaten, it becomes "claqueret." Later, salt, pepper, a dash of vinegar and oil, shallots, chives, and other fresh herbs are added—a delicious treat that it is "always appreciated." This is Léa's version of Cervelle de canuts—it has a slight bite that comes from the addition of horseradish.

The day before, remove the cheese from its container and put it on a piece of cheesecloth stretched tightly over a large bowl. Place in the refrigerator for 24 hours to strain.

The next day, beat the cheese until it becomes smooth and silky.

Wash and dry the chives. With a pair of scissors, snip the chives onto the cheese. Peel and crush the garlic. Stir the garlic and horseradish into the cheese.

Season with salt and freshly ground pepper and mix well. Drizzle with a little vinegar and serve very fresh.

Serves 4

1¼ pounds/500 g farmer's cheese

1 bunch of fresh chives

2 garlic cloves

½ teaspoon creamed or grated fresh horseradish

dash of red wine vinegar

salt and freshly ground black pepper

Preparation time:
the day before, 5 minutes;
on the day, about 15 minutes
Straining: 24 hours

La mère Léa

Vinegar chicken

For best results when cooking this Lyons specialty, you should use a high-quality, free-range chicken and as old an oak-aged red wine vinegar as you can find. Léa would serve Poulet au vinaigre with creamy baked macaroni, but you could also serve it with buttered fresh egg noodles.

Serves 4

1 × 3¼ pound/1.5 kg chicken, quartered, giblets reserved

4 garlic cloves

2 shallots

2 tablespoons vegetable oil

1 tablespoon tomato paste

1¼ cups/300 ml red wine vinegar

4 cups/1 liter chicken stock

1 tablespoon cornstarch

⅔ cup/150 ml heavy cream

1 tablespoon tarragon vinegar

salt and freshly ground black pepper

Macaroni cheese, to serve (see page 143)

Preparation time: 15 minutes

Cooking time: about 50 minutes

Pull off and set aside any pieces of fat on the chicken quarters. Peel and finely chop the garlic cloves and shallots.

Put the chicken fat or half the vegetable oil in a flameproof casserole over medium heat. Add the garlic and shallots and cook until translucent. Add the tomato paste and cook, stirring constantly, for a few minutes. Add the red wine vinegar. Cook until reduced and syrupy. Add the chicken stock. Bring to a boil, then reduce the heat.

Season the chicken pieces. Heat the remaining oil in a skillet and cook the chicken until the pieces are lightly browned all over. Remove the chicken and drain on paper towels, then transfer the chicken to the casserole. Bring to a boil. Reduce the heat, cover, and simmer for 20 minutes.

Remove the chicken pieces from the casserole and keep warm.

Crush the chicken heart and liver with a fork, add them to the sauce, and bring to a boil. Dissolve the cornstarch in a little cold water and whisk it into the sauce. Add the cream and the tarragon vinegar and bring the sauce back to a boil. Immediately reduce the heat and simmer gently for several minutes.

Strain the sauce through a fine-meshed strainer onto the chicken pieces. Serve the chicken immediately with a side dish of Macaroni cheese.

La mère Léa

Baked cardoon with bone marrow

The cardoon is a popular winter vegetable not only in Lyons, but also in Provence, where it is a traditional part of Christmas dinner. This somewhat unfashionable vegetable is from the same family as the globe artichoke. Like the artichoke, it does not keep well. Prepare Gratin de cardons à la moelle on the day you are going to serve it.

Wear gloves when handling cardoons as their juice will blacken your fingernails. Pull off the hard green stems, keeping only the tender white part of the cardoon. With a sturdy knife, peel the stalks carefully, removing any stringy parts.

Fill a large bowl with cold water. Cut the stems into ¾-inch/2-cm pieces and immediately add them to the water to prevent them from turning black.

Bring 8 cups/2 liters of water to a boil in a large stainless steel pan (do not use an aluminum pan). Dice the suet or salted butter. Add a handful of coarse salt, the suet or salted butter, and the drained cardoons to the pan. Cook for 1 hour, until the stems yield to gentle pressure.

Melt the sweet butter in a pan, stir in the flour and cook, stirring constantly until it starts to brown. Add about 2¼ cups/500 ml of the cardoon cooking liquid. Whisk to combine and simmer for about 10 minutes, stirring occasionally. Taste and adjust the seasoning, if necessary.

Drain the cardoons, arrange them in a shallow, ovenproof dish, and pour the sauce over them. Sprinkle the top with the bread crumbs and cheese. Bake in a preheated oven, 400°F/200°C/gas mark 6, for about 15 minutes.

Meanwhile, blanch the marrow bone in boiling water for a couple of minutes. Drain the bone and remove the marrow. Cut the cylinder of marrow into slices. Take the cardoons out of the oven and arrange the marrow slices over the top. Return the dish to the oven for a further 5 minutes. Serve immediately.

Serves 4

6½ pounds/3 kg fresh cardoons or 2¼ pounds/1 kg, peeled and prepared cardoons

1½ tablespoons/20 g beef suet or lightly salted butter

¼ cup/50 g sweet butter

½ cup/50 g all-purpose flour

2 tablespoons dried bread crumbs

1 cup/120 g grated Swiss cheese

1 large marrow bone

coarse salt, fine salt, and freshly ground black pepper

Preparation time: 45 minutes
Cooking time: about 1 hour 40 minutes

La mère Léa

Macaroni cheese

Gratin de macaronis was Léa's son Gaby's favorite. Léa would be furious and throw one of her famous tantrums if a customer dared to leave some of "his" gratin uneaten. It is best to make this dish with thin macaroni.

Bring a large pan of water to a boil, then add a handful of coarse salt and the oil. Add the macaroni. When the water returns to a boil, stir the macaroni with a wooden spoon to keep it from sticking together, and cook for 3 minutes.

Meanwhile, pour the milk and the cream into a pan. Bring to a boil over low heat, then remove the pan from the stovetop.

Melt the butter in another pan. Add the flour and cook, stirring constantly, for a few minutes. Add the hot cream and milk and whisk vigorously. Season to taste.

Drain the macaroni and refresh under cold running water. Stir the macaroni into the simmering sauce and cook for about 4 minutes, depending on the thickness of the macaroni, until it is just tender.

Pour the macaroni and sauce into a shallow, flameproof dish, spreading it out evenly. Sprinkle the top evenly with the grated cheese. Brown the macaroni under a preheated broiler. As soon as the top is golden brown and bubbling, remove from the broiler, and serve.

Serves 4

1 tablespoon vegetable oil
1¾ cups/200 g short macaroni
1¼ cups/300 ml milk
scant 1 cup/200 ml heavy cream
3 tablespoons/40 g sweet butter
2 tablespoons all-purpose flour
scant ½ cup/40 g grated Swiss cheese
coarse salt, fine salt, and freshly ground black pepper

Preparation time: 5 minutes
Cooking time: about 20 minutes

La mère Léa

Roast leg of lamb
with pineapple

Léa would marinate the leg of lamb in red wine lees. These are the dregs that collect in the bottom of the vat during winemaking. Once the winemaker has drawn off the wine, he collects the lees. Léa would use the powerful and aromatic lees produced from the finest wines in her marinade and this would give Gigot à l'ananas a flavor similar to venison.

Serves 8

1 × 4 pounds/1.8 kg leg of lamb
4 cups/1 liter full-bodied red wine
2 shallots
1 large onion
2 cloves
1 bouquet garni
2 fresh sage leaves
2 tablespoons brandy
1 tablespoon vegetable oil
5 black peppercorns
1 pineapple
2 tablespoons/30 g sweet butter
½ teaspoon cornstarch
salt and freshly ground black pepper

Preparation time: 20 minutes
Marinating: 48 hours
Cooking time: about 45 minutes

Two days before cooking, place the lamb in a deep, nonmetallic dish and sprinkle with salt. Pour in the red wine. Peel the shallots and the onion. Cut the onion in half and insert a clove into each half. Put the shallots and onion halves into the dish with the bouquet garni tied with sage leaves, the brandy, vegetable oil, and black peppercorns. Cover and marinate in the refrigerator for 48 hours.

When you are ready to cook, remove the lamb from the marinade and pat thoroughly dry with paper towels. Reserve the marinade. Place the lamb in a roasting pan and roast in a preheated oven, 475°F/240°C/gas mark 9, turning the leg occasionally so that it browns evenly. When the leg is browned, reduce the oven temperature to 400°F/200°C/gas mark 6.

Baste the lamb well with the reserved marinade, adding the vegetables. Cook the lamb for 35 minutes more, if you like your meat rare, or 45 minutes more if you like it medium-rare. Baste frequently with the marinade, using a bulb baster if possible.

Meanwhile, make the pineapple compote. Cut off the top and the base of the pineapple. Peel it, then, using a small, sharp knife, remove the "eyes." Quarter the pineapple lengthwise and remove the fibrous core. On a cutting board with a channel to catch any juices, cut the flesh into small pieces.

Melt the butter in a skillet over low heat. Add the pineapple and brown in the butter, then add the juice. Cover and simmer until the pineapple is cooked and the juices have become syrupy. Season with black pepper.

Strain the remaining marinade into a pan. Bring to a boil over low heat. Dissolve the cornstarch in a little water. Whisk the cornstarch paste into the marinade. Simmer gently, stirring constantly, until it thickens. Adjust the seasoning.

Remove the leg of lamb from the roasting pan. Let it rest, covered with a piece of foil, for about 10 minutes. Carve the meat and arrange on a serving dish. Collect any juices that run and add them to the sauce. Serve immediately with the pineapple compote.

La mère Léa

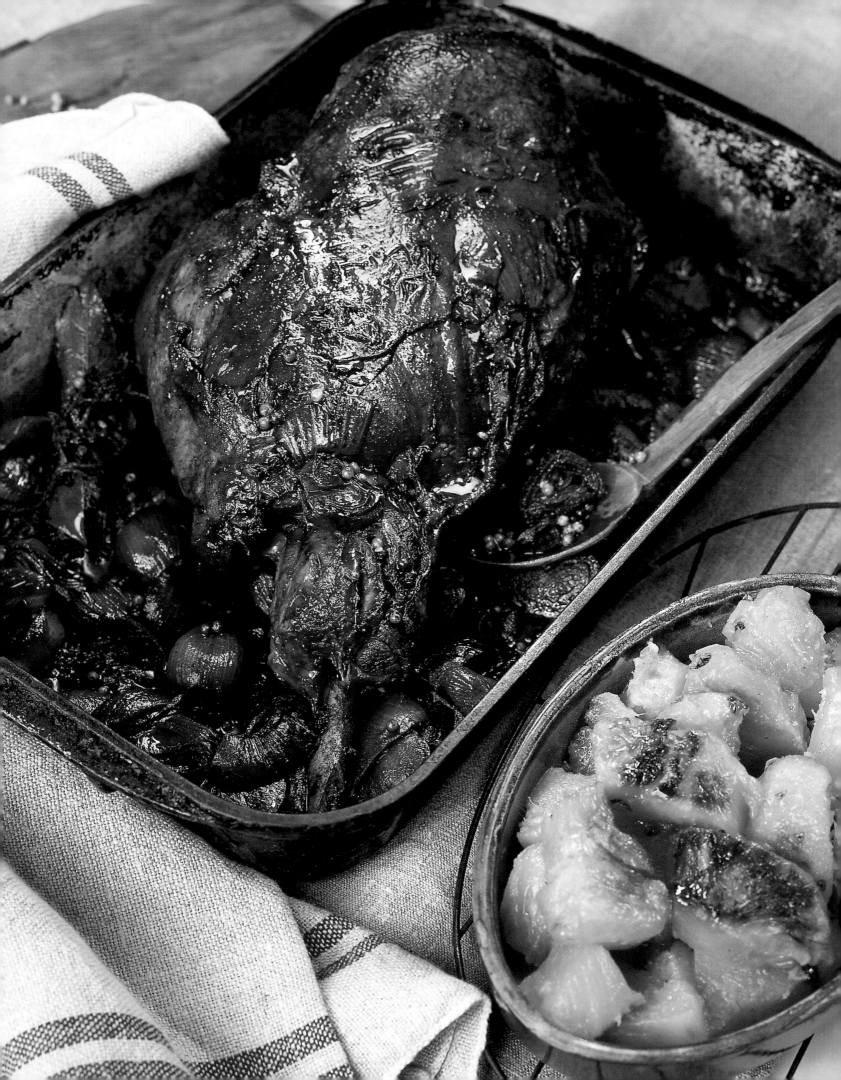

Duck stew

Léa was careful to remove all the excess fat from the poultry that she used for her Civet de canard. She would both brown the bird in this fat and use it to cook the vegetables that would accompany it. Adding the blood to thicken the sauce at the end of the recipe is a delicate operation—the sauce can easily separate. It is best to have the sauce in the top of a double boiler or in a heatproof bowl over barely simmering water before adding the blood.

Serves 4

1 Barbary duck, cut into 4 pieces

1 onion

1 clove

2 garlic cloves

2 shallots

4 cups/1 liter full-bodied red wine

1 bouquet garni

5 black peppercorns

5 juniper berries

¼ cup/50 g sweet butter (optional)

½ cup/120 ml brandy

2¾ cups/250 g pearl onions

5 ounces/150 g fatty bacon, about 5 thick strips or 10 thin strips

4½ cups/300 g white mushrooms

1 cup/250 ml duck blood or beurre manié (made by blending 4 tablespoons all-purpose flour with 2 tablespoons/30 g softened sweet butter)

1 tablespoon chopped fresh flat leaf parsley

salt and freshly ground pepper

Preparation time: 25 minutes

Marinating: 48 hours

Cooking time: 1 hour

Two days in advance, pull the excess fat off the duck pieces and reserve if you like. Peel the onion and insert a clove into it. Peel the garlic and shallots. Pour the wine into a sauté pan and add the onion, garlic, shallots, bouquet garni, peppercorns, and juniper berries. Bring to a boil over low heat. Season the pieces of duck with salt and add them to the marinade. Remove the pan from the heat. Cover and let cool, then chill for 48 hours.

When you are ready to cook, take the duck pieces out of the marinade and pat dry thoroughly on paper towels. Put a spoon of duck fat or butter into a flameproof casserole and melt over high heat. Add the duck pieces and cook until golden on all sides. Add the brandy and set alight.

Strain the marinade into the casserole and bring to a boil over medium heat. Lower the heat and simmer gently for 20 minutes. Remove the duck breasts and keep warm. Simmer the thighs for 20 minutes more.

Peel the pearl onions, place in a pan, and cover with cold water. Season to taste. Tuck a buttered piece of baking parchment over them and cook over low heat until almost all the water has evaporated.

Dice the bacon and bring a pan of water to a boil. Add the bacon and as soon as the water returns to a boil, drain well. Melt a spoon of duck fat or butter in a skillet, add the bacon, and cook until browned.

Trim and rinse the mushrooms, then pat dry. Dice finely and add to the bacon with the remaining butter. Stir, then cook for about 5 minutes. Drain the pearl onions and add them to the skillet.

Remove the duck thighs from the casserole. Reduce the cooking liquid over low heat. Whisk a small ladleful of the liquid into the duck blood. Pour the mixture back into the pan, whisking constantly: Do not let the sauce boil. Alternatively, whisk in the beurre manié, in small pieces at a time. Return the duck pieces to the sauce.

Arrange the duck in a deep serving dish. Spoon the mushroom mixture over the top. Pour in the sauce and garnish with finely chopped flat leaf parsley. Serve immediately.

La mère Léa

Normandy quiche with bacon and andouille sausage

Annette Poulard would, naturally, make this Quiche normande au lard et à l'andouille using the famous andouille sausage made in nearby Vire, its birthplace. It is firm yet soft—a delicious sausage redolent of the woods, salt marshes, and valleys of Normandy, according to Curnonsky, the so-called Prince of Gastronomes. Smoked for one or two months over a gently burning beech wood fire, Vire andouilles are sent to market only when they are deemed to be perfectly smoked.

Butter a loose-based, fluted quiche pan, then line it with the puff pastry. Prick the base with a fork, trim any excess pastry, and crimp the edges. Chill the pie shell for at least 30 minutes.

Dice the bacon. Put the dice into a pan, cover with cold water, and cook over low heat until the water just begins to simmer. Drain and thoroughly dry the bacon with paper towels. Remove the skin from the andouille sausage, then cut it into small dice. In a bowl, combine the bacon and the pieces of andouille.

Break the eggs into a bowl and beat them. Season with a little salt if you like (the bacon and andouille are already quite salty) and pepper. Add the cream and whisk until thoroughly combined.

Sprinkle the bacon and andouille pieces evenly over the pie shell. Pour in the cream and egg mixture. Bake in a preheated oven, 350°F/180°C/gas mark 4, for 35 minutes.

Remove the quiche from the pan. Serve hot with a salad on the side.

Serves 6

1 tablespoon/15 g sweet butter

1¼ pounds/500 g puff pastry

7 ounces/200 g smoked bacon, in a single piece

9 ounces/250 g Vire andouille sausage

3 eggs

2¼ cups/500 ml heavy cream

salt and freshly ground black pepper

salad, to serve

Preparation time: 15 minutes

Chilling: 30 minutes

Cooking time: about 40 minutes

La mère Poulard

Scallop packages
with leeks

A dish of great delicacy, Luté de Saint-Jacques aux poireaux combines the subtlety of scallops with the more robust flavor of vegetables. When the puff pastry shells are cut open, they release an incredible aroma.

Serves 4

16 large scallops and their shells

1 carrot

3 leeks, white parts only

¼ black radish

3¾ ounces/100 g ceps

1 bunch of fresh chives

¼ cup/50 g butter

7 tablespoons fish stock (see page 122)

7 tablespoons heavy cream

all-purpose flour, for dusting

7 ounces/200 g puff pastry

1 egg yolk

coarse salt, fine salt, and freshly ground black pepper

Preparation time: 20 minutes

Cooking time: about 25 minutes

Ask your fishmonger to remove the scallops from their shells and to give you both the top and bottom shells.

Remove the corals and use for another dish. Wash the scallops under cold running water. Remove the black vein and the tough muscle along the side, if necessary. Slice each scallop in half horizontally.

Scrub 4 of the empty shells—lower and upper shells— under cold running water.

Peel and wash the carrot, leeks, and black radish. Cut them into fine batons. Clean the ceps with damp paper towels and slice them thinly. Chop the chives.

Melt half the butter in a sauté pan over very low heat. Add the vegetable batons, season with salt and pepper, cover, and sweat in the butter for about 10 minutes.

Pour the fish stock into a pan over medium heat and bring to a boil until slightly reduced. Add the cream and bring back to a boil. Whisk in the remaining butter. Remove the pan from the heat and adjust the seasoning.

Divide the vegetables between the deeper (lower) half-shells. Spoon a few slices of cep into each shell, and divide the scallops among them. Top each shell with 2 tablespoons of the sauce and a sprinkling of chopped chives. Place the shallow half-shell on top.

On a floured work surface, roll out the puff pastry and cut it into 4 long strips, each about 2 inches/5 cm wide.

Brush the edges of the shells with water. Wrap a strip of pastry around each shell and pinch the ends to seal at the back, where the shell was connected. Seal the pastry package shut with your fingertips. Trim any excess pastry. Beat the egg yolk with a little water and brush it over the pastry.

Make a bed of coarse salt on a cookie sheet and wedge the shells into it. Bake in a preheated oven, 475°F/240°C/gas mark 9, for 8 minutes. The scallops will continue to cook after they are taken out of the oven.

Make a little bed of coarse salt on each of 4 individual serving plates and place a scallop package on top. Your guests will break open the puff pastry crust at the table and inhale the extraordinary aroma of the steamed scallops.

La mère Poulard

Turbot in beurre blanc

Turbot is sometimes called the "pheasant" of the sea because it is so firm and fleshy. Turbot poached in slightly salted milk and crowned with bay leaves used to be the traditional Ash Wednesday dish for wealthy Normandy farmers. Mère Poulard would always keep a milk court-bouillon on the go on her coal-fired stove for Turbotin au beurre blanc.

Peel the shallots, but leave them whole. Put them into a small pan and add the sugar, water, and butter. Cover and gently sweat the shallots over very gentle heat until there is almost no liquid left.

Peel the potatoes and boil them in lightly salted water for about 20 minutes, until tender. Check to see that they are cooked by piercing them with the point of a knife. Drain and keep warm.

Meanwhile, pour about 4 cups/1 liter water and the milk into a large sauté pan. Add the peppercorns, star anise, and lemon juice and bring to a boil. Add the pieces of fish and poach over low heat for 10 minutes.

Meanwhile, make the sauce. Dice the butter. Peel and finely chop the shallots. Put the shallots in a pan with the white wine and simmer over low heat until there is almost no liquid left. Whisk in the butter, 1 piece at a time. Season with salt and pepper. Strain the sauce through a fine-meshed strainer and keep it warm in a bain marie or heatproof bowl set over a pan of barely simmering water.

Chop the chives. Carefully transfer the pieces of fish onto a warmed serving platter. Arrange the potatoes beside them. Sprinkle with chopped chives and garnish with the shallots. Serve immediately with the sauce.

aServes 4

10 shallots

pinch of sugar

1 cup/250 ml water

1½ tablespoons/20 g
butter, diced

2¼ pounds/1 kg potatoes

1¼ cups/300 ml milk

5 black peppercorns

1 star anise

juice of 1 lemon

1 small turbot, brill, or halibut
weighing about 2½ pounds/
1.2 kg, trimmed and cut into
4 pieces

1 bunch of fresh chives

salt

For the sauce

6 tablespoons/80 g sweet butter

2 shallots

scant 1 cup/200 ml dry
white wine

salt and freshly ground
white pepper

Preparation time: 15 minutes
Cooking time: about 40 minutes

La mère Poulard

Brittany lobster stew

As well as Civet d'homard à la bretonne, Mère Poulard would also make Normandy lobster stew, that is, with cream and mushrooms. Today, Mère Poulard's restaurant serves lobsters caught only from the nearby Chausey Islands. They can be seen swimming in the restaurant's tank, their claws tied firmly shut with heavy elastic bands. Chausey lobsters have a particularly strong iodine flavor and very delicate meat.

Serves 4

2 live lobsters weighing about
1 pound 5 ounces/600 g each

1 carrot

1 onion

3 garlic cloves

¼ cup/50 ml vegetable oil

1½ tablespoons tomato paste

5 tablespoons dry white wine,
such as Sauvignon Blanc

1 bay leaf

1 fresh thyme sprig

3 tablespoons brandy

scant 1 cup/200 ml fish stock
(see page 122)

pinch of cayenne pepper

¼ cup/50 ml heavy cream

1½ tablespoons/20 g
sweet butter

2 fresh tarragon sprigs

salt and freshly ground pepper

Preparation time: 20 minutes
Cooking time: about 15 minutes

Kill the lobsters by inserting the point of a sharp knife between the antennae or anesthetize by freezing them for a few hours. On a cutting board, cut the tails of the lobsters into medallions using the segment joints as a guide. Cut the heads in half, remove and discard the stomach sacs. Break off the claws and crack them with a hammer. Collect the lobster coral and put it and the green tomalley (liver) into a bowl. Alternatively, you can plunge the lobsters into salted boiling water for 1 minute, drain, and then cut up.

Peel and finely dice the carrot and the onion. Peel the garlic cloves and crush them with a garlic press.

Pour the oil into a large sauté pan over high heat. Add the pieces of lobster. As soon as the shells turn red, remove the pan from the heat and pour out the oil. Return the pan to the heat and add the diced vegetables, garlic, tomato paste, white wine, bay leaf, and thyme. Cook, stirring constantly, for a few minutes. Pour in the brandy and set alight.

When the flames have died down, add the lobster coral and tomalley mixture and the fish stock. Bring to a boil over medium heat, then reduce the heat, and simmer very gently for about 6 minutes. Season with salt, freshly ground pepper, and cayenne pepper.

Transfer the lobster pieces to a warmed serving dish and keep warm. Return the pan to the heat and add the cream. Then whisk in the butter, in small pieces at a time. Remove and discard the herbs, bring the sauce to a boil, and pour it over the lobster.

Chop 1 tarragon sprig. Sprinkle the lobster with the chopped tarragon, garnish with the tarragon sprig, and serve.

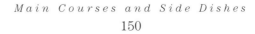

La mère Poulard

Leg of lamb
en croûte

In Brittany, sheep are grazed on the extensive intertidal salt-marshes, the "prés-salés." The flesh of a "pré-salé" lamb has a unique flavor, enhanced by all the sea salt it has consumed. It is greatly prized. Mère Poulard would cook a classic roast leg of lamb on Sundays. She would also serve Gigotin d'agneau de pré-salé en croûte because she enjoyed making puff pastry, for which she would use freshly churned, slightly salted butter.

Serves 8

1 × 4 pound/1.8 kg leg of lamb
1 carrot
1 large onion
½ leek, white part only
1 cup/250 ml dry white wine
1 tablespoon all-purpose flour
½ teaspoon tomato paste
½ bunch thyme
¼ cup/50 ml olive oil
2 shallots
1¼ pounds/500 g puff pastry
1 egg yolk
1½ tablespoons/20 g slightly salted butter
salt and freshly ground pepper

To serve

1¾ pounds/800 g green beans
3 tablespoons/40 g butter
coarse salt

Preparation time: 30 minutes
Cooking time: about 3 hours

Ask your butcher to bone the leg of lamb and cut it into 8 equal slices. Also ask him to chop up the bones.

Put the bones into a roasting pan and brown them in a preheated oven, 425°F/220°C/gas mark 7, for 20–30 minutes.

Peel and dice the carrot and onion. Dice the leek and add to the roasting pan with the carrot and onion. Cook for 10 minutes.

Remove the pan from the oven. Reserve ¼ cup/50 ml of the wine and add the remainder to the roasting pan. Stir well to scrape up any sediment on the base.

Transfer the bones and the liquid to a pan. Stir in the flour and tomato paste and pour in just enough cold water to cover the bones. Cover the pan and simmer for about 2 hours, until syrupy.

Meanwhile, season the meat with salt and pepper and sprinkle with some of the thyme leaves. Heat the oil in a skillet, add the meat, and cook over high heat until browned on both sides. Remove the meat from the skillet, set aside, and let cool.

Peel the shallots and slice them into rounds. Pour the fat out of the skillet and return it to the heat. Add the shallots and a sprig of thyme, and cook, stirring constantly, for a few minutes. Add the remaining white wine, stirring to scrape up any sediment. Bring to a boil and cook until slightly reduced, then add to the pan with the bones. Collect any cooking juices that have run from the lamb and add to the pan.

Cut the puff pastry into 8 pieces. Roll out each piece into a rectangle slightly larger than twice the size of the lamb slices. Place a slice of lamb on a rectangle. Wrap the dough around the meat and seal the edges with a brush dipped in cold water. Repeat for all the slices of lamb.

Line a cookie sheet with baking parchment. Place the pastry-wrapped lamb slices, spaced slightly apart, on the parchment. Beat the egg yolk with a little water and brush this over the pastry. Bake in a preheated oven, 425°F/220°C/gas mark 7, for about 8 minutes for rare meat, or for 10–12 minutes for medium.

Trim the green beans. Cook them in lightly salted boiling water for 8 minutes, then drain. Just before serving, melt the butter over low heat and toss the beans in it for a few minutes.

Remove the lamb from the oven and transfer to a wire rack to rest for 5 minutes. Strain the stock in the pan through a fine-meshed strainer into a clean pan. Cut the butter into small pieces and whisk it into the stock over medium heat. Pour this gravy into a sauceboat. Serve the lamb on a bed of green beans and hand the gravy separately.

La mère Poulard

Veal steaks with Livarot cheese

Livarot is Normandy's oldest cheese. J.B. Pommereu de la Bretesche recorded that it was being eaten in Paris as long ago as 1693. Mère Poulard used fresh unripened Livarot for Noix de veau au livarot, as younger cheese is softer and not so strong.

Peel the carrot and onion and cut them into large pieces. Melt 2 tablespoons/30 g of the butter in a pan over medium heat and cook the vegetables for a few minutes. Pour in the vermouth and cook until slightly reduced, then add the crème fraîche. Bring to a boil, then lower the heat, and cook until the liquid is reduced by half. Strain the sauce through a fine strainer into a clean pan and set aside.

Cut the cheese into sticks. Using the point of a sharp knife, insert the cheese sticks into the veal steaks. Trim any rind from the bacon. Wrap each steak in a strip of bacon and tie with kitchen string. Season with salt and pepper.

To make the garnish, cut off any tough spinach stems, wash the leaves in cold water, and pat dry. Melt the salted butter in a skillet over low heat. Add the spinach and stir. Season with salt and pepper. Cook for about 8 minutes, stirring occasionally.

Meanwhile, heat the oil in a skillet over high heat. Add the veal steaks and cook until browned on all sides. Lower the heat and cook for 4 minutes more on each side.

Reheat the sauce. Dice the remaining butter and whisk it into the sauce, a little at a time. Pour it into a sauceboat. Arrange the veal steaks in the middle of a serving dish, surround with the spinach, and serve immediately with the cream sauce.

Serves 4

1 carrot
½ onion
7 tablespoons/100 g sweet butter
7 tablespoons dry vermouth
1¼ cups/300 ml crème fraîche
½ Livarot cheese (or other semisoft, washed rind cheese), about 4 ounces/125 g
4 thick veal round steaks weighing about 6 ounces/180 g each
4 bacon strips
¼ cup/50 ml peanut oil
salt and freshly ground black pepper

For the garnish
3¼ pounds/1.5 kg spinach
3 tablespoons/40 g slightly salted butter
salt and freshly ground pepper

Preparation time: 25 minutes
Cooking time: about 20 minutes

La mère Poulard

Meringue cake
with custard

Gâteau de neige à la crème anglaise is a novel way of preparing the classic floating islands dessert. The light meringue is cooked in a caramel-lined charlotte mold instead of being poached in individual portions. Adrienne would make this daily for her dessert trolley.

Serves 8

10 sugar lumps

1 cup/250 ml water

12 eggs

1 tablespoon vanilla sugar

generous 1 cup/210 g
superfine sugar

1 vanilla bean

4 cups/1 liter milk

Preparation time: 5 minutes

Cooking time: about 35 minutes

Put the sugar lumps and water in a pan and cook over medium heat until a rich brown caramel forms. Pour the caramel into a charlotte mold and swirl it around so that it coats the side and base of the mold (hold the mold with potholders).

Separate the eggs. Set the yolks aside. Whisk the egg whites until they are almost stiff. Whisk in the vanilla sugar and 2 heaping tablespoons of the superfine sugar. Continue beating until the egg whites are stiff.

Transfer the meringue to the prepared mold. Tap the mold gently on the counter to settle the mixture. (In the home kitchen, it may be easier to do this in two batches.)

Fold a few sheets of old newspaper and place them in a roasting pan or shallow ovenproof dish. This will keep the base of the meringue from overcooking. Place the charlotte mold on top of the newspaper and fill the roasting pan or dish with enough hot water to come halfway up the side of the mold. Place the pan in a preheated oven, 300°F/150°C/gas mark 2, for 7 minutes. Raise the oven temperature to 350°F/180°C/gas mark 4 and cook for 7–8 minutes more.

Remove the meringue from the oven and immediately run a sharp knife around the edge of the mold. Unmold the meringue into a deep dish—it should come away easily. Chill in the refrigerator.

To make the custard, split the vanilla bean lengthwise and place in a heavy pan with the milk. Bring to a boil. Meanwhile, using an electric mixer, beat the egg yolks with the remaining sugar until frothy and pale yellow. Beating constantly, pour the hot milk into the eggs in a thin stream. Return the custard to the pan. Remove the vanilla bean and scrape the seeds into the custard. Have a bowl of ice water ready.

Return the pan to low heat. Cook gently, stirring constantly, until the custard is thick enough to coat the back of a wooden spoon—do not let it boil, or it will curdle. When it is ready, plunge the base of the pan into the ice water to stop further cooking.

When the custard has cooled to room temperature, chill in the refrigerator until ready to serve.

Pour the custard into a bowl and serve it with the meringue.

La mère Adrienne

Peach omelet

A luscious dessert, Omelette aux pêches evokes happy childhood memories. Half omelet, half cake, it is best served hot or warm. Adrienne would make the omelet at the beginning of the meal service, cover it with foil, and keep it warm in a very low oven. You could vary the omelet using other summer fruits, such as apricots, nectarines, or plums.

Serves 4

⅔ cup/150 ml evaporated milk

7 tablespoons heavy cream

1 unwaxed lemon

generous ¾ cup/100 g all-purpose flour

generous ½ cup/100 g superfine sugar

2 teaspoons baking powder

5 eggs

1 tablespoon kirsch

generous ½ cup/125 g butter

4 ripe peaches

salt

Preparation time: 15 minutes

Resting: 30 minutes

Cooking time: about 20 minutes

Combine the evaporated milk and cream. Wash and dry the lemon, then finely grate the rind into a large bowl. Sift in the flour, then add the sugar, a pinch of salt, and the baking powder. Mix thoroughly and make a well in the center. Separate 2 of the eggs and add 3 whole eggs and 2 egg yolks to the well. Reserve the whites. Beat the eggs and gradually incorporate them into the flour. Pour in the milk mixture and stir to a smooth batter. Stir in the kirsch.

Beat the egg whites until stiff, but not dry and gently fold them into the batter. Cover with a dishtowel and let rest for 30 minutes.

Reserve 2 tablespoons of the butter and melt the remainder in a skillet over very low heat. Fold the melted butter into the batter.

Cut a cross into the base of the peaches and plunge them into boiling water for 30 seconds. Refresh in cold water. Peel the peaches. Cut them in half, remove the pits, and cut the flesh into dice or thin slices.

Heat the reserved butter in a nonstick skillet until it sizzles. Add the peaches and cook gently, turning them over to make sure they are evenly colored. Pour all the batter into the skillet at once. Shake and tilt the skillet to make sure that the batter is evenly distributed. When the edges begin to set, push them toward the center with a spatula. Cook for about 7 minutes until the underside is set and golden brown.

Place a plate that is the same size as the skillet over the omelet and invert the two. Slide the omelet back into the skillet to cook the other side. Cook for 5 minutes more. Slide the omelet onto a warmed serving dish and serve immediately.

La mère Adrienne

Grand-Marnier soufflés

Everyone knows a soufflé cannot stand around … the guests are waiting! Marthe and Fernande Allard would serve this light Soufflé chaud au Grand-Marnier all year round. It was always a delicate operation since the temperature of the unreliable coal-fired range had to be judged exactly. Because each soufflé was made from scratch, it had to be ordered at the beginning of the meal. The finished soufflé was dusted with confectioners' sugar and taken straight to the waiting customer.

Lightly grease 6 ramekins or 1 large soufflé dish with 1½ tablespoons of the butter. Sprinkle with superfine sugar and shake to coat. Pour out any excess. Put the ramekins into the refrigerator.

Bring the milk to a boil in a pan. Separate the eggs.

Heat the remaining butter over very low heat. When it is half-melted, remove the pan from the heat. Stir gently until completely melted.

Pour the butter into a large bowl and sift the flour over it. Gradually add the hot milk, stirring to combine. Whisk in the egg yolks, sugar, and Grand-Marnier.

Whisk the egg whites with a pinch of salt until stiff. With a wooden spoon or rubber spatula, fold half of the egg whites into the Grand-Marnier mixture. Then, gently fold in the remainder.

Divide the soufflé mixture among the ramekins, so that they are about two-thirds full; otherwise the soufflés will overflow.

Immediately transfer the ramekins to a preheated oven, 350°F/180°C/gas mark 4, and cook for about 15 minutes. (A single large soufflé will take about 25–30 minutes.)

Put the confectioners' sugar in a small strainer. Remove the soufflés from the oven, dust with the sugar, and serve immediately.

Serves 6

1 cup/220 g sweet butter
1⅓ cups/260 g superfine sugar, plus extra for dusting
2¼ cups/500 ml milk
6 eggs
generous ¾ cup/140 g all-purpose flour
3 tablespoons Grand-Marnier
1 tablespoon confectioners' sugar
salt

Preparation time: 20 minutes
Cooking time: about 20 minutes

Les mères Allard

Chocolate charlotte

This delicious Charlotte au chocolat is very easy to make. It is best to buy ladyfingers from a bakery (or to make them at home) as store-bought ones tend to be inferior. It is also worth taking the time to cut the chocolate into small pieces with a knife, as it will melt quicker and more evenly, so reducing the risk of burning. Marthe would serve this charlotte with a rich custard.

Serves 8

4 ounces/125 g semisweet chocolate (at least 55% cocoa solids)

6 tablespoons superfine sugar

3 eggs

scant 1 cup/200 g sweet butter

2¼ cups/500 ml water

7 tablespoons rum

about 20 ladyfingers

salt

vanilla custard, to serve

Preparation time: about 30 minutes, the day before

Cooking time: about 10 minutes

Prepare the charlotte the day before serving. Using a sharp knife, finely chop the chocolate. Put the pieces in a heatproof bowl, drizzle with 2 tablespoons warm water, and add 3 tablespoons of the sugar.

Set the bowl over a pan of barely simmering water and gradually melt the chocolate. Do not let the base of the bowl touch the surface of the water.

Separate the eggs. Beat the yolks into the melted chocolate with a hand-held electric mixer. Continue beating until the eggs are fully incorporated and the mixture is smooth and shiny.

Remove the bowl from the heat. Dice the butter into small pieces. With the mixer running, gradually beat the butter into the chocolate mixture, 1 piece at a time.

Whisk the egg whites with a pinch of salt until stiff. Add half the egg whites to the chocolate mixture, beating fairly vigorously with a wooden spoon or rubber spatula. Fold in the remaining egg whites.

Pour the water into a pan. Add the rum and the remaining sugar and bring to a boil, stirring until the sugar has dissolved. Boil until the mixture is reduced by half. Remove the pan from the heat and let cool.

Line a charlotte mold with plastic wrap, leaving an overhang to make unmolding easier. Cut one end of each ladyfinger at an angle. Dip them into the rum syrup and arrange them like the spokes of a wheel in the base of the mold. Next, line the sides of the mold.

Pour in the chocolate mousse and smooth the surface with a spatula. Arrange a layer of dipped ladyfingers over the mousse. Place a small plate on top of the charlotte and weigh it down (use 1–2 cans of tomatoes). Chill overnight.

The next day, invert a serving dish over the mold and, holding the two firmly together, reverse. Unmold the charlotte, peel off the plastic wrap, and serve with a bowl of fresh vanilla custard.

Les mères Allard

Apple tart

Marthe and Fernande Allard would make this Tarte aux pommes when Reinette apples were in season. The layer of apple filling contrasts superbly with the crisp pastry below and the caramelized apple topping.

Serves 6–8

For the rough-puff pastry

generous 1 cup/250 g butter, plus extra for greasing

1 tablespoon lard or shortening

5 cups/500 g all-purpose flour, plus extra for dusting

¼ teaspoon salt

7 tablespoons water

For the filling

2¼ pounds/1 kg eating apples

juice of ½ lemon

7 tablespoons water

⅔ cup/125 g sugar

For the topping

2–3 eating apples

juice of ½ lemon

Preparation time: the day before, 15 minutes; on the day, 40 minutes

Cooking time: about 1 hour

Start making the tart the day before serving. To make the pastry, let the butter and lard or shortening soften to room temperature, then dice. Reserve a handful of flour and sift the remainder into a large bowl. Add the butter and lard or shortening. and sprinkle in the salt. Rub in the fat until the mixture resembles bread crumbs. Drizzle the water into the bowl and lightly work the mixture into a dough. Briefly knead gently. Gather the dough into a ball and dust with the reserved flour. Cover with a dishtowel and chill overnight.

Next day, remove the dough from the refrigerator and roll out on a lightly floured counter into a long rectangle. Fold the top third of the rectangle down to the middle and the bottom third up, like a letter, and rotate it a quarter turn. Roll out the dough again into a long rectangle and fold in thirds as before. Form it into a ball.

Lightly grease a 9-inch/23-cm loose-based tart pan. Roll out the dough to a round about ⅛ inch/3 mm thick and large enough to fit the pan. Lift the dough into the pan, gently press it into the sides, and trim any excess.

Prick the base with a fork and place the tart shell in the refrigerator.

To make the filling, peel, quarter, and core the apples. Toss in the lemon juice, cut into slices, and place in a pan. Add the water, cover, and cook over low heat for 15 minutes. Add a little more water if necessary. Add the sugar and stir until it has dissolved. Cover and cook for 5 minutes more. Transfer the cooked apples to a large bowl and let cool completely.

To make the topping, peel, quarter, and core the apples. Toss in the lemon juice, then slice thinly.

Spread a ½-inch/1-cm thick layer of the apple filling in the tart shell. Arrange the apple slices over the filling in concentric circles. Cook the tart in a preheated oven, 400°F/200°C/gas mark 6, for about 40 minutes, until the pastry is crisp and the apple topping lightly browned. Cover the tart with a piece of foil if the apple looks likely to burn before the pastry is cooked.

Remove the tart from the oven. Transfer it from the tart pan to a wire cooling rack. Serve warm.

Les mères Allard

Floating islands with pink praline

Île flottante aux pralines roses, a light dessert, which can also be made in ramekins, was devised by Paulette Blanc using fresh Bresse eggs and pink praline from Saint-Genix. It could be served with brioche or chocolate cake.

Grease a large soufflé dish with the butter and coat it with a fine layer of sugar, tipping out any excess. Roughly crush the praline in a mortar with a pestle.

Separate the eggs. Set the yolks aside. Whisk the egg whites with a pinch of salt until stiff. Sprinkle in the sugar and whisk until the meringue is shiny. Fold in the crushed praline.

Spoon the meringue into the dish. Place in a roasting pan and add hot water to come halfway up the side of the dish. Bake in a preheated oven, 300°F/150°C/gas mark 2, for about 20 minutes. Test by gently pressing the surface. If it is not sticky, the meringue is cooked. Remove from the oven, let cool, then unmold it onto a serving dish.

To make the custard, pour the milk into a pan. Split the vanilla bean lengthwise and add it to the pan with generous ½ cup/100 g of the sugar. Bring to a boil over low heat.

Meanwhile, add the remaining sugar to the egg yolks. Beat until pale yellow and a ribbon trail forms when the whisk is lifted.

Remove the vanilla bean from the milk. Pour the hot milk into the egg mixture in a slow, steady stream, beating constantly.

Pour the custard into a clean pan and cook over low heat, stirring constantly, until just simmering. Plunge the base of the pan into a bowl of cold water to stop further cooking. Stir for 1 minute. Strain the custard through a fine-meshed strainer into a bowl and let cool, then cover, and chill in the refrigerator.

Serve the floating island in a small pool of custard and hand the remaining custard separately. Serve with brioche or sponge cake if you like.

To make the pink praline, put ⅓ cup/50 g blanched almonds or hazelnuts in a pan with ⅓ cup/75 g superfine sugar, 4 tablespoons water, and a drop of pink food coloring. Bring to a boil over high heat, swirling the pan to dissolve the sugar. Boil, without stirring, for 5 minutes. Immediately pour onto an oiled cookie sheet and let cool.

Serves 6

1½ teaspoons sweet butter

scant 1 cup/175 g superfine sugar, plus extra for sprinkling

3¼ ounces/80 g pink praline (see method for homemade praline)

7 eggs

salt

For the custard

4 cups/1 liter milk

1 vanilla bean

1¼ cups/250 g superfine sugar

3 egg yolks

Preparation time: 15 minutes

Cooking time: about 20 minutes

La mère Blanc

Desserts

Swiss chard pie

A traditional Niçoise dessert, Tourte aux blettes, is made using the green leaves of Swiss chard. The "little chard" native to Nice has small, lighter green, leaves and is available in local markets all the year round. However, it is not available outside the region.

The day before serving, wash the golden raisins and put them in a bowl. Cover with warm water and set aside to soak overnight.

Next day, let the butter soften to room temperature. Wash and dry the lemon and finely grate the rind.

To make the dough, tip the flour onto a large wooden board and sprinkle the salt on top. Make a well in the center and add the softened butter, lemon rind, eggs, sugar, milk, and rum. Mix well, then sprinkle with the baking powder. Knead the dough until smooth and elastic. Cover with a dishtowel and let rest for 1 hour at room temperature.

To make the filling, cut off and discard the Swiss chard stems. Wash the leaves, then blanch them in a large pan of boiling water for 1 minute. Drain and refresh under cold water. Drain again, pat the leaves dry, then finely chop them.

Drain the golden raisins. Combine the chopped leaves with the raisins, pine nuts, apricot jelly, and rum or orange-flower water in a large bowl.

Brush a cookie sheet with oil.

Halve the dough. Roll out 1 piece on a lightly floured counter into a rectangle or round. Keep the other piece of dough covered until required. Drape the dough over the rolling pin and transfer it to the prepared cookie sheet.

Spread a ¾-inch/2-cm thick layer of chard filling over the dough, leaving a border all around. Peel and core the apples, then slice thinly. Arrange the slices over the filling.

Roll out the second piece of dough and lay it over the filling. Press down around the edges to seal, creating a thin rim of pastry.

Lightly beat the egg in a small bowl. Brush the pie with the beaten egg.

Bake in a preheated oven, 425°F/220°C/ gas mark 7, for about 35 minutes. Check the pie from time to time.

Remove the pie from the oven and generously dust the top with superfine sugar. Transfer to a wire rack to cool. The pie will keep for several days if stored in a cool place, but not in the refrigerator. According to Mère Barale, this Swiss chard pie actually tastes better slightly stale.

Serves 8

For the dough

scant 1 cup/200 g sweet butter

½ unwaxed lemon

5 cups/500 g all-purpose flour, plus extra for dusting

1½ teaspoons salt

2 eggs

generous ½ cup/100 g superfine sugar, plus extra for dusting

4 tablespoons milk

1 tablespoon rum

4 teaspoons baking powder

vegetable oil, for brushing

1 lightly beaten egg, to glaze

For the filling

¾ cup/100 g golden raisins

2¼ pounds/1 kg Swiss chard

scant 1 cup/100 g pine nuts

½ cup/100 g apricot jelly

4 tablespoons rum or orange-flower water

3 large apples

Preparation time: 40 minutes

Soaking: 24 hours

Cooking time: about 35 minutes

Resting: 1 hour

La mère Barale

Orange cake

Elisa was taught this recipe for Gâteau à l'orange by her mother Virginie. Wearing a white cap and always smiling, Virginie would often help her daughter in the kitchen. Caramel ice cream or a frozen Grand-Marnier mousse would complement this delicate cake, which can be frosted or left plain.

Serves 6

2 unwaxed oranges

generous ½ cup/150 g unsalted butter, plus extra for greasing

¾ cup/150 g superfine sugar

2 eggs

1 cup/115 g all-purpose flour, plus extra for dusting

2 teaspoons baking powder

1 cup/115 g confectioners' sugar

1 tablespoon kirsch

Preparation time: 15 minutes

Cooking time: 30 minutes

Wash and dry the oranges. Grate the rind, taking care not to grate any of the bitter white pith. Chop finely if necessary.

Melt the butter in a pan over very low heat. Remove the pan from the heat and stir in the superfine sugar until the mixture is smooth. Squeeze the juice from 1 orange and strain it into the butter and sugar mixture through a fine strainer. Beat in the eggs, 1 at a time.

Sift the flour into a bowl and stir in the baking powder, then add the dry ingredients to the pan and stir to combine. Reserve 1 tablespoon of the grated orange rind for decoration and fold in the remainder.

Grease and flour a 9½-inch/24-cm cake pan. Pour the cake batter into the pan. Bake in a preheated oven, 425°F/220°C/gas mark 7, for 10 minutes. Lower the oven temperature to 350°F/180°C/gas mark 4 and bake for 20 minutes more.

Remove the cake from the oven and let cool in the pan. Place a wire rack over a piece of baking parchment and turn the cake out onto the rack.

Sift the confectioners' sugar into a bowl. Squeeze the juice from ½ orange and strain it into the sugar. Add the kirsch and stir until smooth.

Spread the frosting over the top and sides of the cooled cake with a long metal spatula. Decorate with the reserved rind. Let the frosting set before transferring the cake to a serving dish.

La mère Blanc

Sugar galette

Georges Blanc has always kept this unusual recipe for Galette au sucre in his repertoire. He inherited it from his maternal grandfather, who had a bakery in Vonnas. The originality of the recipe lies in baking the brioche dough with a layer of whipped cream spread on top.

The day before serving, sift the flour into a bowl. Add a pinch of salt and the sugar and crumble in the yeast. Add the eggs, 1 at a time, then knead the dough until it pulls away from the side of the bowl.

Cut the butter into small pieces, add them to the bowl, and continue to knead until the dough pulls away from the side again. Set the bowl of dough aside at room temperature to rest for 45 minutes. Cover with a dishtowel or oiled plastic wrap and chill overnight in the refrigerator.

The next day, line a cookie sheet with baking parchment. Shape the dough into a ball and place it in the center. Flatten it with the palm of your hand until it forms a round about ¼ inch/5 mm thick. Cover with a dishtowel and set aside to rise in a draft-free place for about 2 hours.

When the dough has doubled in bulk, roll up the edges to create a ½-inch/1 cm rim. Prick the center of the round with a fork.

Lightly beat the egg and brush the rim with it. Make sure that the glaze does not drip onto the cookie sheet as any drips will prevent the dough from rising in the oven.

Chill a large bowl in the freezer for about 3 minutes. Remove it, pour in the chilled cream, and whip it. Using a spatula, spread the whipped cream evenly over the dough round and dust the top with the sugar. Bake in a preheated oven, 475°F/240°C/gas mark 9, for 10–15 minutes. Check to see if it is cooked by gently lifting the edge with a spatula. The base of the galette should be lightly browned.

Slide the galette onto the wire rack and allow it to cool a little before serving.

Serves 4

For the brioche dough

scant 1½ cups/170 g all-purpose flour

1½ tablespoons superfine sugar

¼ ounce/7 g fresh yeast

2 eggs

7½ tablespoons sweet butter

salt

For the topping

1 egg

scant 1 cup/200 ml heavy cream, chilled

1½ tablespoons superfine sugar

Preparation time:
the day before, 20 minutes;
on the day, 20 minutes

Resting: 2 hours

Chilling: 12 hours

Freezing: 3 minutes

Cooking time: about 15 minutes

La mère Blanc

Pink praline ice cream

Glace aux pralines roses was one of Mère Bourgeois' specialties. Lassagne, chef to Marshal César de Choiseul, Count Plessis-Praslin, first devised the idea of roasting almonds together with sugar. The caramelized result, a specialty of Montargis, has been popular since 1630. The small towns of Aigueperse in Puy-de-Dôme and Vabres-l'Abbaye in Aveyron were also involved in the manufacture of praline, selling it in little paper cones.

Makes 4 cups/1 liter

7 ounces/200 g pink praline (for homemade praline, see page 163)

2¼ cups/500 ml heavy cream

2¼ cups/500 ml milk (Mère Bourgeois specifies raw, unpasteurized milk, which generally has a better flavor)

12 egg yolks

2 cups/400 g granulated sugar

individual meringues, to serve (optional)

Preparation time: 15 minutes
Cooking time: about 20 minutes

Crush the pink praline in a mortar with a pestle. Pour the cream and milk into a pan with the crushed praline and bring to a boil over low heat.

Meanwhile, beat the egg yolks with the sugar until they are pale yellow and form a ribbon trail when the beaters are lifted. Beating constantly, pour the hot milk into the eggs in a thin, steady stream.

Transfer the custard to a clean, heavy pan. Half fill a large bowl with ice water and set it near the stove. Cook the custard over low heat, stirring constantly. When it is thick enough to coat the back of a wooden spoon, remove the pan from the heat. Immediately plunge the base into the ice water to prevent the custard from cooking any more. Stir for several minutes. Chill the custard thoroughly before freezing it in an ice cream maker.

The pink praline ice cream can be stored in the freezer, but its texture will be best if it is served as soon as it has firmed up.

Using 2 spoons, place a scoop of ice cream on chilled individual plates. Sandwich the ice cream between 2 meringues (see page 173) if you like.

La mère Bourgeois

Meringues

Mère Bourgeois would bake light and airy meringues with the egg whites left over from making pink praline ice cream (see page 170). She claimed that for the best results when making meringues, the egg whites should be left at room temperature for two days. This causes the whites to liquefy, making it much easier to beat a great deal of air into them.

Put the egg whites into a large, grease-free bowl. Beat them with an electric mixer set at medium speed. Gradually increase the speed. When the egg whites have doubled in volume, sprinkle in half the sugar. Continue beating until smooth, shiny peaks form. Sprinkle the remaining sugar over the egg whites and fold in using a rubber spatula.

Line a cookie sheet with baking parchment and stick the parchment in place with a drop of meringue on each corner.

Drop tablespoonfuls of meringue onto the cookie sheet, spacing them well apart. Alternatively, use a pastry bag with a large tip to shape the meringues.

Bake in a preheated oven, 250°F/120°C/gas mark ½, for 2 hours. Turn the oven down to its lowest setting and cook for at least another 6 hours. You can leave the meringues in the oven, with the heat turned off and the door ajar, to dry overnight.

Transfer the meringues to a wire rack to cool completely. They will keep fresh for several days if stored in an airtight container. Serve with wild strawberries or other berries folded into whipped cream or with sherbets and ice creams, including pink praline ice cream.

Makes about 12

9 ounces/250 g egg whites (about 5 large or extra large eggs)

2¾ cups/500 g superfine sugar

Preparation time: 15 minutes

Cooking time: about 8 hours

La mère Bourgeois

Choux puffs with pastry cream

Choux à la crème, little puffs, filled with luscious pastry cream and coated with crisp golden caramel, would be on Mère Bourgeois' menu every day. If they are baked as soon as the dough is ready, they are less likely to crack as they cook.

Makes about 10 puffs

For the dough

1 cup/250 ml milk

1 cup/250 ml water

scant 1cup/200 g best-quality sweet butter

1½ teaspoons salt

1½ teaspoons sugar

2⅔ cups/300 g all-purpose flour

7 eggs

For the pastry cream

2¼ cups/500 ml milk

1 vanilla bean

6 egg yolks

¾ cup/150 g superfine sugar

⅓ cup/40 g all-purpose flour

1 tablespoon rum or kirsch (optional)

1 pat of butter

For the caramel

generous ½ cup/100 g superfine sugar

1 tablespoon water

juice of ½ lemon

Preparation time: 20 minutes

Cooking time: about 40 minutes

To make the dough, pour the milk and water into a pan. Dice the butter and add it to the pan with the salt and sugar. Bring to a boil over low heat.

Sift the flour into a bowl. Remove the pan from the heat and add the flour, all at once, to the boiling liquid. Beat vigorously with a wooden spoon. Return the pan to the heat and stir the mixture until the dough begins to pull away from the side of the pan.

Beat in the eggs, 1 at a time. Make sure each egg has been fully incorporated before adding the next.

Line a large cookie sheet with baking parchment, sticking the corners with small pieces of dough. Drop spoonfuls of the dough onto the parchment, spacing the puffs well apart to allow room for them to expand during baking. Alternatively, use a pastry bag with a large tip.

Bake in a preheated oven, 425°F/220°C/gas mark 7, for 10 minutes. Wedge the oven door ajar with a spoon to keep the puffs from deflating, lower the temperature to 400°F/200°C/gas mark 6, and cook for 10 minutes more.

Transfer the cooked puffs to a wire rack to cool.

To make the pastry cream, pour the milk into a pan. Split the vanilla bean lengthwise, scrape the seeds into the pan, and drop the bean into the milk. Bring the milk to a boil, then remove the pan from the heat, and set aside.

Beat the egg yolks with the sugar until they are pale yellow and form a ribbon trail when the beaters are lifted. Beat in the flour. Beating constantly, pour the hot milk into the egg mixture in a thin, steady stream. Pour the pastry cream into a clean, heavy pan. Cook over low heat, stirring, until it begins to boil. Remove the pan from the heat and discard the vanilla bean. If you like, stir in the rum or kirsch. Melt a pat of butter over the surface of the cream to prevent a skin from forming and let cool.

To make the caramel, put the sugar into a heavy pan. Add the water and 2 drops of lemon juice. Cook over medium heat until the sugar caramelizes and develops a rich brown color. Remove the pan from the heat.

Holding each puff by the base, dip the top into the caramel. As they are dipped, put the puffs, caramel side down, onto a cookie sheet lined with baking parchment.

To serve, make a slit in the base of each puff. Spoon the pastry cream into a pastry bag and fill each of the puffs. The puffs should be eaten on the day that they are made and within 2 hours of filling.

La mère Bourgeois

Bresse galettes

These crisp Galette bressane always accompanied the vanilla ice cream with hot chocolate sauce served in Eugènie Brazier's restaurant in Lyons and at the hilltop restaurant in Luère. Mère Brazier first made the galettes while still living in her native region of Bresse. She also baked them for the Milliat family in Lyons for whom she worked as a maid and cook in 1914, but it is almost certain that she used less butter in those days!

Make 2 galettes, each serving 6 people

¾ cup/175 ml milk

¼ ounce/10 g fresh yeast

5 cups/500 g all-purpose flour

1 heaping tablespoon granulated sugar

6 eggs

1⅓ cups/300 g best-quality sweet butter, softened, plus extra for greasing

salt

For the topping

7 tablespoons sweet butter

1 cup/200 g superfine sugar

Preparation time:
the day before, 40 minutes;
on the day, 20 minutes
Cooking time: about 30 minutes

The day before serving, gently warm the milk until it is lukewarm. Crumble the yeast into it and stir until completely dissolved.

Sift the flour into a large bowl. Sprinkle in a pinch of salt and the sugar. Make a well in the center and break the eggs into it. Add the yeast mixture and stir to combine.

Dice the butter and add it to the dough. Knead vigorously for at least 15 minutes. Cover the bowl with a dishtowel and set aside to rise at room temperature for at least 1 hour, until it has doubled in bulk.

Punch down the dough and knead for 5 minutes. Cover with a dishtowel and chill in the refrigerator overnight.

Next day, grease 2 × 10-inch/25-cm loose-based tart pans with a little butter.

Knead the dough again, then cut it in half. Roll 1 half into a round to fit a tart pan. Use a rolling pin to help transfer the dough to the pan. Repeat with the remaining dough. Cover with dishtowels and leave to rise in a draft-free place for at least 1 hour.

For the topping, dice the butter and dot about 15 pieces on each galette. Sprinkle with the sugar.

Bake both the galettes in a preheated oven, 425°F/220°C/gas mark 7, for about 30 minutes. Remove the cooked galettes from the tart pans and place on a wire rack to cool completely.

Serve the galettes, warm or cold, with a cup of coffee or vanilla ice cream and hot chocolate sauce.

La mère Brazier

Carrot sherbet

One day in May 1979, Gisèle Crouzier was trying to devise a refreshing and unusual sherbet. Since it was not a very good season for fruit, she invented this original and delicious sherbet made from carrots and spiked with tangerine liqueur. Sorbet à la carotte is still served between courses at her restaurant as a palate cleanser.

Peel the carrots and cut them into large pieces. Place them in a pan and pour in sufficient cold water to cover. Bring to a boil over medium heat. Lower the heat, cover, and simmer for about 20 minutes, until tender.

Drain the carrots, reserving the cooking liquid. Purée the carrots in a food mill and set aside. Alternatively, process in a food processor and rub through a wire strainer to remove any coarse fibers.

Pour 2¼ cups/500 ml of the reserved cooking liquid into a heavy pan. Add the sugar and stir over low heat until it has dissolved. Bring to a boil and boil, without stirring, for 2 minutes more, then remove the pan from the heat.

Stir the carrot purée into the syrup. Add the orange and lemon juices, crème fraîche, and liqueur. Mix thoroughly. When the mixture is cool, pour it into an ice cream maker and freeze according to the manufacturer's instructions.

Place one scoop of sherbet in each individual ice cream dish. Drizzle with a little extra liqueur and serve with wafers.

Makes 2¼ cups/500 ml sherbet

2¼ pounds/1 kg carrots, about 14–18 carrots

2¾ cups/500 g sugar

⅔ cup/150 ml orange juice

4½ tablespoons lemon juice

4 tablespoons crème fraîche

7 tablespoons tangerine liqueur, such as Mandarine Napoléon, plus extra for drizzling

wafers, to serve

Preparation time: 10 minutes
Cooking time: about 25 minutes

La mère Crouzier

Warm apple pastry

Feuilleté chaud aux pommes was one of the few desserts made by Paulette Castaing. She enjoyed making puff pastry and she loved the flavor of Reinette apples. The apples would keep for several months in one of the restaurant's cellars. If you do not have the time or the inclination to make your own puff pastry, you can use ready-made, but if it is frozen, thaw it first.

Serves 6

6 firm eating apples

juice of 1 lemon

6 tablespoons/80 g butter

2¼ teaspoons superfine sugar

1 egg yolk

confectioners' sugar, to decorate

scant 1 cup/200 ml sweetened crème fraîche, to serve

For the puff pastry

1¾ cups/200 g all-purpose flour, plus extra for dusting

7 tablespoons water

scant 1 cup/200 g sweet butter

salt

For the pastry cream

1 cup/250 ml milk

½ vanilla bean

3 egg yolks

scant ⅓ cup/75 g superfine sugar

3 tablespoons cornstarch

6 tablespoons water

1½ teaspoons sweet butter

Preparation time: 30 minutes

Resting time: about 3 hours

Chilling: 30 minutes

Cooking time: about 50 minutes

La mère Castaing

To make the pastry, sift the flour into a bowl, make a well in the center, and add the water and a pinch of salt. Lightly knead into a dough, gather into a ball, and chill for 20 minutes.

Place the butter between 2 sheets of plastic wrap. Pound with a rolling pin to flatten it into a rectangle about 5 × 4 inches/ 13 × 10 cm. Roll out the dough on a lightly floured surface to a 15 × 5-inch/38 × 13-cm rectangle. Place the butter in the center of the dough. Fold the top third down and the bottom third up, then rotate a quarter turn Roll the dough into a rectangle again, fold into thirds, and chill for 20 minutes. Repeat the process of rolling, folding, and rotating four more times, chilling in between the processes for 20 minutes each time.

To make the filling, peel, quarter, and core the apples. Sprinkle with lemon juice and put them into an ovenproof dish. Dot with the butter and sprinkle with the sugar. Bake in a preheated oven, 350°F/180°C/gas mark 4, for 15 minutes. Remove the dish from the oven, set aside to cool, and then chill in the refrigerator.

To make the pastry cream, pour the milk into a heavy pan. Split the vanilla bean, add it to the milk, and bring to a boil over low heat. Meanwhile, beat the egg yolks with the sugar until pale yellow and the whisk leaves a ribbon trail when lifted. Dissolve the cornstarch in the water and whisk it into the eggs. Pour the boiling milk into the egg mixture in a thin, steady stream, whisking

constantly. Pour the custard into a clean pan. Cook over low heat, stirring constantly, until it just begins to boil. Remove the pan from the heat and discard the vanilla bean. Melt the butter on the surface of the pastry cream or float a sheet of plastic wrap to prevent a skin from forming. Let cool.

Halve the dough. Thinly roll one half into a rectangle and trim the edges. Line a cookie sheet with baking parchment. Lift the rectangle of pastry onto the cookie sheet with the rolling pin. Prick the pastry all over with a fork, then spread it with a thin layer of pastry cream, leaving a margin at the edges. Arrange the cold apple quarters over the pastry cream.

Roll the remaining dough into a rectangle a little larger than the first. Brush the edges of the apple-covered pastry with a little water. Lay the second rectangle over the apples and press the edges together to seal. Chill for 20 minutes.

With a sharp knife, make criss-cross lines over the top of the pastry. Beat the egg yolk with a few drops of water and brush over the pastry. Take care not to let the glaze drip onto the cookie sheet, as it would prevent the puff pastry from rising.

Bake in a preheated oven, 425°F/220°C/ gas mark 7, for about 20 minutes. Two minutes before the end of the cooking time, sift confectioners' sugar over the top. When cooked, the pastry should have a golden caramelized color. Serve hot with lightly sweetened chilled crème fraîche.

Caramelized apple tart

Tarte solognote is not quite the same as a Tarte Tatin. The Tatin sisters cooked their tart entirely on top of their old range in their restaurant near Sologne in the Loire Valley. This meant that the caramelized juices from the apples would bubble up and over the pastry as it cooked. Gisèle Crouzier recalls an exhausting Sunday when customer demand dictated that she produce forty-two portions of Sologne tart. What a feat!

Serves 6

For the pastry

1¾ cups/200 g all-purpose flour, plus extra for dusting

generous ½ cup/125 g butter, diced

1 egg

2–3 tablespoons superfine sugar

1–2 tablespoons milk (optional)

salt

For the topping

generous ½ cup/125 g sweet butter

⅔ cup/125 g granulated sugar

2¼ pounds/1 kg eating apples

crème fraîche, to serve (optional)

Preparation time: 30 minutes

Resting: 1 hour

Cooking time: about 45 minutes

To make the pastry, sift the flour into a bowl. Make a well in the center and add the butter, egg, sugar and a pinch of salt. Lightly work together to form a dough. If it is too dry and crumbly, add a little milk. Form the dough into a ball, wrap it in a dishtowel, and chill for at least 1 hour.

To make the topping, dice the butter and sprinkle it evenly over the base of a high-sided copper cake pan, a *tarte tatin* pan, or an ovenproof skillet. Cover the base of the pan with a ½-inch/1-cm deep layer of granulated sugar.

Peel, quarter, and core the apples. Stand the apple quarters on their sides in the sugar, leaving a small space between them.

Place the cake pan or skillet on very low heat, cover, and simmer gently for about 35 minutes, until the apples are translucent and bathed in a melted butter and sugar mixture. Increase the heat under the pan or skillet and cook until the juices caramelize.

Meanwhile, on a lightly floured surface, roll out the pastry into a thin round large enough to cover the cake pan or skillet. Place it over the apples and trim any excess from around the edges. Bake in a preheated oven, 425°F/220°C/gas mark 7, until the pastry is golden.

Invert the cooked tart onto a wire rack and let cool slightly. Serve it warm with crème fraîche, if you like.

La mère Crouzier

Pears poached in red wine

Poires à la confiture de vin rouge is served cold. Gisèle Crouzier found that she had the best results when she used flavorsome, tender pear varieties, such as Louise-Bonne, Conference, or Williams. Sometimes, she would serve the wine-poached pears with a velvety custard sauce.

Serves 6

2¼ cups/500 ml red wine

1 cup/250 ml water

1 cup/200 g superfine sugar

pinch of ground cinnamon

1 clove

6 Williams pears

freshly ground black pepper

Preparation time: 10 minutes
Cooking time: about 30 minutes

Pour the wine and water into a pan. Add the sugar, cinnamon, clove, and a little pepper. Gradually bring to a boil over medium heat, then reduce the heat to a gentle simmer.

Peel the pears—do not break off the stems. Drop the pears into the simmering wine and poach them for about 20 minutes over low heat.

Using a slotted spoon, remove the cooked pears from the wine and arrange them in a glass bowl.

Return the pan to the heat and boil the poaching liquid until it is thick enough to coat the back of a wooden spoon. Pour the sauce over the pears. Chill before serving.

La mère Crouzier

Orange layer cake

Léa did not offer her customers an extensive dessert menu, but this Biscuit à l'orange, a few types of fruit salad (made from the morning's purchases at the Quai Saint-Antoine market), and a fluffy lemon sherbet were always available. It is best to keep the finished cake for one or two days before serving so that the layers will not separate when it is sliced.

Two days before serving, put the unpeeled oranges into a large pan full of cold water. Bring to a boil, then drain, and refresh in cold water. Keep the oranges immersed in a bowl of cold water for 24 hours. Change the water twice during this time.

The day before, drain the oranges and pat them dry with paper towels. On a cutting board with a channel to catch the juices, cut the oranges in half, then into thin slices. Put the orange slices and all the juice into a pan. Add the sugar and cook for about 35 minutes, stirring frequently. Remove the candied orange slices from the heat and let cool.

To make the pastry cream, pour the milk into a pan. Split the vanilla bean lengthwise, add it to the pan, and bring to a boil over low heat.

With an electric mixer, beat the eggs and egg yolks with the sugar until pale and the whisk leaves a ribbon trail when lifted. Stir in the flour with a wooden spoon. Whisking constantly, pour the boiling milk into the egg mixture in a thin, steady stream. Pour the custard into a clean, heavy pan, set over low heat, and cook, stirring, until thickened. Melt the butter over the surface of the pastry cream to prevent a skin from forming. Chill in the refrigerator.

Stir the Grand-Marnier into the pastry cream and fold in the candied orange slices. Cut the sponge cake horizontally into three layers. Put the bottom layer on a cake rack and spread it with half the orange pastry cream. Put the second layer on top and cover with the remaining cream. Top with the remaining layer.

Break the chocolate into small pieces. Combine the chocolate with the coffee in the top of a double boiler or in a heatproof bowl set over a pan of barely simmering water. Stir until melted. Immediately spread the chocolate over the top and sides of the cake. Let the chocolate set, then transfer the cake to a serving dish. Store in a cold place, but not the refrigerator, for at least 12 hours before serving.

Serves 6–8

4 unwaxed oranges

1 cup/200 g sugar

1 génoise sponge cake (from your bakery or homemade)

3¾ ounces/100 g bittersweet chocolate

5 tablespoons strong coffee

For the pastry cream

2¼ cups/500 ml milk

1 vanilla bean

2 eggs

2 egg yolks

generous ½ cup/100 g sugar

⅓ cup/40 g all-purpose flour

1½ teaspoons sweet butter

5 tablespoons Grand-Marnier

Preparation time:

the day before, 20 minutes

Soaking: 24 hours

Cooking time: about 40 minutes

Resting: about 12 hours

La mère Léa

Camembert fritters

Mère Poulard and most Normandy farmers' wives often made Beignets de camembert, coating pieces of the cheese in a hard cider batter. The French gastronome Brillat-Savarin, who declared that Camembert was the perfect way to end a meal, would no doubt have adored these fritters.

Serves 4

¼ ounce/10 g fresh yeast

1¾ cups/200 g all-purpose flour

1 cup/250 ml hard cider

1 ripe Camembert

oil, for deep-frying

salt and freshly ground pepper

To garnish

1 Batavia or escarole lettuce

1 shallot

½ bunch of fresh chives

For the vinaigrette

3 tablespoons peanut oil

1 tablespoon red wine vinegar

salt and freshly ground pepper

Preparation time:

about 15 minutes

Cooking time: about 4 minutes

Crumble the yeast into a little lukewarm water and stir to dissolve. Sift the flour into a bowl, make a well in the center, and pour in the cider and the dissolved yeast. Using a wooden spoon, gradually incorporate the flour into the liquid. Season the batter with salt and pepper.

Separate the salad greens, wash, and dry. Peel and thinly slice the shallot. Chop the chives. Whisk all the vinaigrette ingredients in a salad bowl. Add the salad greens, chives, and shallot slices and toss lightly.

Cut the Camembert in 12 equal pieces. Pour the oil into a pan to a depth of about 4–6 inches/10–15 cm or into a deep-fryer. Heat the oil to 350°F/180°C, or until a spoon of batter dropped into the pan rises to the surface in a few seconds. Dip each piece of cheese into the batter and drop it into the hot oil. Fry 3 fritters at a time.

When the fritters are golden, remove them with a slotted spoon and drain on paper towels. Keep warm while you cook the remaining fritters. Serve with the salad.

La mère Poulard

Rhubarb frangipane tart

In June, rhubarb has a sharp, lemony flavor, but stalks harvested in September tend to be more bland. Mère Poulard would cook the rhubarb separately and serve the cooking juices in a bowl with slices of the Tarte normande meringuée à la rhubarbe. If you like, you can soak the peeled stalks in cold water for a few hours to reduce the rhubarb's acidity.

Serves 6

2¼ pounds/1 kg rhubarb

scant ½ cup/80 g sugar

confectioners' sugar, for dusting

For the pâté sucré

generous 1 cup/125 g all-purpose flour, plus extra for dusting

generous ¼ cup/60 g superfine sugar

¼ cup/50 g sweet butter, plus extra for greasing

1½ teaspoons slightly salted butter

1 egg

salt

For the frangipane

¼ cup/50 g sweet butter

3 eggs

7 tablespoons sugar

¼ cup/25 g ground almonds

2¼ cups/500 ml heavy cream

Preparation time: 25 minutes

Resting: 2 hours

Cooking time: about 45 minutes

First make the pâté sucré. Sift the flour into a bowl and add the sugar and a pinch of salt. Dice the sweet butter and add it to the bowl with the slightly salted butter and egg. Quickly work the ingredients into a dough. Collect the dough into a ball, cover it with a dishtowel, and place in the refrigerator for at least 2 hours.

Meanwhile, peel and slice the rhubarb. Put it in a pan over low heat. Add a little water and the sugar. Simmer, stirring occasionally, for about 15 minutes. Drain well, reserving the juices.

To make the frangipane cream, melt the butter over very low heat. Remove from the heat as soon as it has melted. Beat the eggs with the sugar until pale and the whisk leaves a ribbon trail when lifted. Gently fold in the ground almonds and cream until thoroughly combined, then fold in the melted butter.

On a lightly floured surface, roll out the dough into a round. Grease a 9-inch/23-cm tart pan with butter and line it with the dough. Trim any excess. Prick the base of the tart shell with a fork, then spread the rhubarb over it. Pour the frangipane cream over the rhubarb and smooth the surface. Bake in a preheated oven, 350°F/180°C/gas mark 4, for 25 minutes.

Take the tart out of the oven. Remove it from the pan and transfer to a wire rack. Dust the top of the tart with confectioners' sugar. Serve the tart while it is still warm, accompanied by a pitcher of the rhubarb cooking juices.

La mère Poulard

Rice pudding with apples

Annette Poulard would make Riz au lait aux pommes every day. She would serve it warm in little earthenware bowls with applesauce on the side. Use a short grain, starchy, rice for this recipe.

Wash the rice in cold water and drain well. Bring 8 cups/2 liters water to a boil in a large pan. Add the rice, bring back to a boil, and cook for 5 minutes. Drain well.

Pour the milk into a heavy pan. Split the vanilla bean lengthwise. Add ⅔ cup/110 g of the sugar, the bay leaf, and vanilla bean to the pan. Gradually bring to a boil over low heat. Stir in the rice and cook over low heat for 30 minutes, checking occasionally that it has not dried out.

Meanwhile, peel, quarter, and core the apples, then cut them into ½-inch/1-cm cubes. Toss in lemon juice. Put the apples into a pan with the butter and water. Add the remaining sugar. Cook over low heat, stirring occasionally, for about 10 minutes.

Remove the bay leaf and vanilla bean from the rice. Scrape the vanilla seeds back into the pan with the tip of a knife and mix well. Serve the rice warm with a side dish of applesauce.

Serves 4

scant 1 cup/150 g short grain rice

4 cups/1 liter milk

1 vanilla bean

¾ cup/150 g superfine sugar

1 bay leaf

4 large eating apples

juice of ½ lemon

1½ tablespoons/20 g butter

1 tablespoon water

Preparation time: 15 minutes

Cooking time: about 45 minutes

La mère Poulard

Glossary

US	UK	US	UK	US	UK
all-purpose flour	plain flour	ham hock	pig's trotter	spiny lobster	crawfish, langouste
apple vinegar	cider vinegar	hard cider	cider (alcoholic)	stovetop	hob
bacon strips	bacon rashers	heaping (spoon)	heaped (spoon)	sugar lumps	sugar cubes
baking parchment	non-stick baking paper	heavy cream	double cream	superfine sugar	caster sugar
		ice water	iced water	sweet butter	unsalted butter
beef chuck	chuck steak	jelly (fruit)	jam (fruit)	Swiss cheese	Gruyère cheese
beef shank	shin of beef	ladyfingers	sponge fingers	tart pan	tart tin
beef short ribs	beef thin ribs	lamb rib chops	lamb cutlets	tip (pastry bag)	nozzle (piping bag)
Belgian endive	chicory	loaf pan	loaf tin	tomato paste	tomato purée
bittersweet chocolate	dark chocolate	mealy (potatoes)	floury (potatoes)	toothpick	cocktail stick
		paper towels	kitchen paper	vanilla bean	vanilla pod
broil, to	grill, to	pastry bag	piping bag	veal rib chops	veal best end chops
broiler	grill	peanut oil	groundnut oil	veal round steak	veal leg fillet
celery root	celeriac	pearl onions	baby or pickling onions	veal rump	veal fillet
cheesecloth	muslin			white mushrooms	button mushrooms
cake pan	cake tin	pit (olives, cherries, etc.)	stone (olives, cherries, etc.)	zucchini	courgette(s)
confectioners' sugar	icing sugar	pitted (olives, cherries)	stoned (olives, cherries)		
cornichons	small gherkins	plastic wrap	cling film		
cornstarch	cornflour	pork blade shoulder	pork spare rib		
counter	worktop	pork fat back	thin slices of pork fat for barding		
crimini mushrooms	chestnut mushrooms				
Dutch oven	large cast-iron casserole with a lid	pork shoulder	pork spare rib		
		pork side	pork belly		
eggs, extra large	eggs, large	portobello mushrooms	field mushrooms		
eggs, large	eggs, medium				
evaporated milk	unsweetened condensed milk	punch down (dough)	knock back (dough)		
farmer's cheese	fromage frais	quiche pan	quiche tin		
fava beans	broad beans	red bell pepper	red pepper		
frosting	icing	roasting pan	roasting tin		
golden raisins	sultanas	salad greens	salad leaves		
green bell pepper	green pepper	scallions	spring onions		
grinder	mincer	semisweet chocolate	plain chocolate		
ham	fresh leg of pork, unless described as smoked or cured, when it equates with ham in the U.K.	sherbet	sorbet		
		shortening	lard		
		skillet	frying pan		
		smoked herring	kipper		

Note

Cuts of meat are not identical in France, the United States, and Britain and some modern butchers no longer produce traditional cuts. Those listed in the recipes and above are the nearest equivalents.

Unless otherwise stated, milk is always full cream and eggs are large (medium in Britain).

Health professionals advise that eggs should not be eaten raw. This book contains recipes made with raw or lightly cooked eggs. Vulnerable people, such as the elderly, invalids, the very young, pregnant and nursing mothers, and those with an impaired immune system are advised to avoid these dishes.

This book contains recipes that include nuts, nut oils, and other nut derivatives. It is advisable for those with known allergic reactions and those who may suspect allergic reactions to substitute other ingredients. Sunflower, safflower, or soy oils are all satisfactory substitutes for peanut oil.

Index

Conversions

Standard cup measurements, tablespoons and teaspoons, imperial measurements where appropriate, and metric measurements are used throughout this book. Use one set of measurements only, as they are not interchangeable.

All cup and spoon measurements are level, unless otherwise stated.
1 tablespoon = 15 ml
1 teaspoon = 5 ml
1 cup = 8 fluid ounces/235 ml

The following charts provide a convenient, at-a-glance conversion, but are not precise.
1 ounce = 28.35 grams
1 pound = 453.59 grams
1 US fluid ounce = 29.57 ml
1 UK fluid ounce = 28.41 ml

Approximate solid measures

Imperial	Metric
¼ ounce	10 g
½ ounce	15 g
¾ ounce	20 g
1 ounce	30 g
1½ ounces	40 g
2 ounces	60 g
3 ounces	80 g
4 ounces	120 g
5 ounces	150 g
6 ounces	175 g
7 ounces	200 g
8 ounces	225 g
9 ounce	250 g
10 ounces	275 g
11 ounces	300 g
12 ounces	350 g
13 ounces	375 g
14 ounces	400 g
15 ounces	425 g
1 pound	450 g
1¼ pounds	500 g
2¼ pounds	1 kg

Cup measurements for solid ingredients will vary depending on the type (i.e. 1 cup flour = 4 ounces/120 g, but 1 cup butter = 1 pound/450 g)

Approximate liquid measures

US	Imperial	Metric
¼ cup	2 fluid ounces	50 ml
½ cup	4 fluid ounces	125 ml
⅔ cup	5 fluid ounces	150 ml
¾ cup	6 fluid ounces	175 ml
1 cup	8 fluid ounces	250 ml
1¼ cups	10 fluid ounces	300 ml
1½ cups	12 fluid ounces	350 ml
1¾ cups	14 fluid ounces	400 ml
2 cups	16 fluid ounces*	475 ml
2½ cups	20 fluid ounces**	600 ml
4 cups	35 fluid ounces	1 liter

* 1 US pint
** 1 imperial pint

Acknowledgments

Many thanks:

especially to Georges Blanc for his passion for the legacy of these 10 exceptional "mères", his appreciation of their profound mark on French cuisine and his enthusiasm for recording their recipes for future generations;

to his team at Vonnas for their warm welcome;

to Philippe Lamboley for having faith in me;

to Florence Lécuyer for her understanding and great professionalism;

to the four great chefs of Lyons: Pierre Orsi (and his father), Christian Bourillot, Jean-Paul Lacombe and Roger Roucou (now retired) who enlightened me on the subject of the Lyons "mères";

to my dear friend Anne-Marie Zorelle for her support and her invaluable help with documentary research;

to Parisian chef Gérard Besson, who introduced me to Adrienne, "la Vieille";

to Adrienne, who kindly took the time to tell me her wonderful story;

to Claude Layrac, present proprietor of Restaurant Allard;

to Jean Montagard, cook and writer, without whose help I should never have made the acquaintance of Mère Barale in Nice;

to Catarina-Elena Barale, the whimsical Mère Barale;

to Gilbert Lombard, past proprietor of Mère Bourgeois' restaurant, who recounted the past with such feeling that my head was filled with images of that mythical place;

to Hervé Rodriguez, current proprietor of Mère Bourgeois' restaurant who, with great flair, showed me how to make the famous warm pâté;

to Jacotte Brazier, Mère Brazier's vivacious granddaughter;

to the Human-Donet family, current proprietors of Beau-Rivage in Condrieu, who introduced me to the world of Mère Castaing;

to Paulette Castaing whose quiet elegance was equaled only by her great talent;

to Michel-Pierre Goacolou, current proprietor of La Croix Blanche Inn;

to Gisèle Crouzier who allowed me to visit her home on several occasions and was kind enough to show me her recipe notebook;

to Philippe Rabatel, current proprietor of Chez Léa, who drew such a vivid picture of the eccentric Léa;

to Éric Vannier, native of Mont-Saint-Michele and current proprietor of Mère Poulard's inn, who is fascinated by the stories recounted by his grandmother about the woman who was her great friend, Annette Poulard;

to Michel Bruneau, cook and writer;

to Marie-France Michalon, stylist, Jean-François Rivière, photographer and Marc Walter, artistic director, who applied their talent to recreating the atmosphere of the Mères' era;

and finally, of course, to my beloved parents, Jean and Madeleine Jobard.

Coco Jobard

Editor: Florence Lecuyer
Graphic Design: Marc Walter

Marie-France Michalon and Jean-François Rivière would like to thank the following shops for their kind contributions: À la mine d'argent, Antheor, Au fond de l'allée, Au puceron chineur, Apilco, Bernard Carant, Caraco, Cuisinophilie, Éric Dubois, Fuchsia, Geneviève and Marie-Dominique Jauzon, Geneviève Lethu, Le Bon Marché, Le Creuset, Mis en demeure, Palais Royal, and finally, Vonnas antique dealer, Jacques Rey.

The editor would like to thank Marine Barbier and Christine Martin for their invaluable help.

Photo credits

All of the photographs are by Jean-François Rivière, with the exception of the photos of documents and the following portraits: p.11, Bac communication—p.16, Joël Michaud—p.17, Roger Bel—p.30, François Roboth—p.35, Raphaël Gatti.